Praise for Bob's 12 Dis

"This is an incredible book. It changes lives in very profound ways, and even more important, the changes are not transient, they stick. I highly recommend this book to anyone who is serious about living a happy, healthy and successful life. Be prepared, you will not be the same afterward!"
Dr. Sharon Rolbin
Author of *Surviving Organizational Insanity*

"This fast-moving and enjoyable book gives you a specific 12-part program you can follow to become the kind of person you want to become and achieve any goal you can set for yourself."
Brian Tracy, Brian Tracy International
Author of *Maximum Achievement* and *Advanced Selling Strategies*

"Success requires discipline. Bob Urichuck sets the example and provides you with the step-by-step approach. Everything you need to live the life of your dreams is included in these 12 Disciplines. Don't just read it, do it!"
Richard Tan, Managing Director,
Success Resources Pte Ltd.

"We can all get more out of lives if we know how. Bob Urichuck's book gives us the blueprint. Read it, follow the guidelines and meet a whole new you."
Patricia Fripp, Past President, National Speakers Association
Author of *Get What You Want*

"A wonderful book! A complete inside-out approach to your success. It is written in a manner that gets you committed first to yourself and to your dreams. It then guides you through a well thought-out process to make your dreams a reality. A great help in finding the discipline and courage you need to soar!"
Lilly Walters, Executive Director,
Walters International Speakers Bureau

"One of the five disciplines required for the foundation of a Learning Organization is 'personal mastery.' Bob's 12 Disciplines provide the means for any learner to mastermind his very own successful journey of non-stop learning, developing and achieving personal triumph."

Helen Wang, Partner
MINDNET, Singapore

"For years I've tried to master self-discipline with books, seminars and re-learning. Reading Bob's 12 Disciplines gave me an instant road map— to organize my priorities. What Bob said in the book reinforces my belief that personal values are more important than hard work. Working hard without a road map leads us to directions all over. Working smart with a goal makes a world of difference!"

Aileen Tan, Executive Director
McKee Fehl Contractors (Asia) Pte Ltd.

"I have read many books of this genre and tire of wading through 500-1000 pages to get to the substance. Your book takes the opposite approach. It is entirely pragmatic and to the point. I much prefer your approach. Anyone who wants to change their life for the better, has the tools immediately available in this book."

John McClelland
Facilities Commercial Realty Inc.

"Life gives us a tool box. Bob Urichuck gives us a tool: the 12 Disciplines. Read it! Use it! Master it! Learn how to make your dreams come true."

W. Mitchell
Author of *It's Not What Happens to You, It's What You Do About It*

December 16, 2005

Elica,

Thanks for taking the time
to meet with me.
May you live the life of
your dreams!

Bob

Bob Urichuck

Online for Life

The 12 Disciplines
for Living Your Dreams

Books that inspire, help and heal

Published by Creative Bound Inc.
P.O. Box 424, Carp, Ontario
Canada K0A 1L0
(613) 831-3641
www.creativebound.com

ISBN 0-921165-65-X
Printed and bound in Canada

This book is a revised edition of the book *The XII Disciplines to Living the Life of Your Dreams: Master Self-Motivation and Personal Leadership* also by Bob Urichuck.

Book design by Wendelina O'Keefe
Photograph by Teckles Photography

printing number 10 9 8 7 6 5 4 3 2 1

Canadian Cataloguing in Publication Data

Urichuck, Robert
        Online for life : the twelve disciplines for living your dreams

Includes bibliographical references.
ISBN 0-921165-65-X

        1. Self-actualization (Psychology) I. Title.

BF637.S4U75 2000   158.1   C00-900327-4

Personal Companion of:

_____

Name

_____

Starting Date

This book is dedicated to my two sons, Michael and David. I am so proud of you. May you each continue to live the life of your dreams.

Acknowledgments ∽

Online for Life represents many years of experience – experience gained through good times and bad times, success and failure, life and death. When I look back, I think appreciatively of the many people who had an impact on my life. There are far too many to mention here but I would at least like to recognize my parents, my in-laws, my friends, neighbors, business associates and clients for their support over the years.

I also acknowledge the inner power that guides me, all the way from idea creating to attracting the people and circumstances to make the ideas a reality. When I left the corporate world to pursue my dream, I knew what I had to do, but I didn't know who was going to be involved and when. I left that to the inner power. Writing this book was one of my goals, and those listed below each played a part in making it a reality.

Years ago when I started to develop my business as an international professional speaker I engaged another professional speaker, Denis Cauvier, to coach me. He provided me with the information and guidance to fast-forward my business. I am most grateful for the expertise that he shared with me. Denis not only encouraged me to write a book, he helped me make it a reality.

To learn more about the speaking business, I joined the Canadian Association of Professional Speakers, where I learned, and shared, experiences with other professional speakers and authors. I am grateful to the members of the Ottawa, Toronto, Calgary, Halifax and Montreal chapters, and the other chapters from across Canada.

After being invited to speak at a Toastmasters conference, I joined Toastmasters International. I learned a lot in a short time. I thank all the members of Luncheon Troupers, District 61, and the Singapore Federation of Toastmasters Clubs. Your support and feedback have made me a better communicator.

Groups of people were instrumental in my progressive success as a professional speaker and author. And then, there is the team behind this book.

In Asia, SNP References Pte Ltd: Tan Poay Lim, publishing manager, and Sin Yoke Yin, editor.

In North America, Creative Bound Inc: Gail Baird, president and publisher, Wendy O'Keefe, designer, and Barbara Clarke, communications and marketing manager.

Each of these publishing houses treated this book with special care. Without their dedication and team spirit, the book would have not been published and made available to you.

Above all, I couldn't have even started without the support and encouragement of my loving wife, Joan, and my two wonderful sons, Michael and David. Not only did they give me the "space," they learned to live without me far too many days, evenings and weekends.

Finally, there is one other person, a person that you may not know as well as you should. That person is you, the reader. The most important person in the world. Without you there would be no reason to write this book. Thank you.

While writing this book I received the support of many organizations and businesses. They showed confidence in me by engaging me to speak, train or consult. I would like to acknowledge and thank them.

Professional Associations
    Canadian Association of Professional Speakers (CAPS),
    Canadian Association of Pre-Retirement Planners (CAPP)
    Canadian Club, Canadian Curling Association (CCA)
    Canadian Council on Health Services Accreditation (CCHSA)
    Canadian Information Processing Society (CIPS)
    Canadian Professional Sales Association (CPSA)
    Canadian Restaurant and Food Association (CRFA)
    Canadian Society of Association Executives (CSAE),
    Canadian Wood Council (CWC)
    Meeting Professionals International (MPI)
    National Golf Course Owners Association (NGCOA)
    Ontario Association for Co-operative Education
    Ottawa-Carleton Board of Trade
    Ottawa-Carleton Home Builders' Association (OCHBA)
    Ottawa Centre for Research and Innovation (OCRI)
    Rotary Club of Bougis Junction, Singapore
    Toastmasters International: Ottawa Luncheon Troupers, Ottawa,
    Les Mots Dits, Cantley, Singapore Federation of Toastmasters Clubs
    Tourism Industry Association of Nova Scotia (TIANS)
    United Way of Ottawa-Carleton

Learning Institutions

Singapore Institute of Management

University of Ottawa

Algonquin College

Institute of Professional Management

Singapore Civil Service College

Canadian Institute of Management

Co-Op Ontario

CPSA Sales Institute

Government/Crown

Office of the Auditor General

Canada Post Corporation

Royal Canadian Mint

Business Development Bank

Cayman Islands Department of Tourism

Indian and Northern Affairs

Canadian Tourism Commission

Export Development Corp

Business

London Life

Mitel Corporation

Dollco Printing

Envirocopy

Wackid Radio

Leon's Furniture Limited

Club de Golf Mont Cascades

Bombardier Motor Corp

Energy Pathways (On-Site)

Corel Corporation

Ski Mont Cascades Water Park

Bay Consulting & Design

Nortel Networks

MindNet, Singapore

Reed Elsevier (Singapore) Pte Ltd.

L. Taylor Enterprises

Ottawa Citizen

Texec

Hotels, Resorts & Cruise Lines

Traders Hotel, Singapore

Royal Crowne Plaza Singapore

Atlific Hotels and Resorts Sheraton Towers, Singapore

Mandarin Court, Singapore

Celebrity Cruise Lines

Costa Cruise Lines

Magazines—Published Articles

HR Today

Golf Business Canada

Industry Canada – Strategis

Sharing Ideas

Manager

Small Business Canada

National Capital Region Executive

Today's Manager

Everybody's Business

Contents ⌐

Introduction ⌒

We all have dreams, but in order to make these dreams into reality it takes an awful lot of determination, self-discipline and effort.

Jesse Owens

Do you know who you are? Do you love what you are doing? Do you have what you want out of life? Do you *know* what you want out of life? Do you wake up and jump out of bed every morning eager to face the challenges of a new day? If not, then this book will position you as "online for life," inspiring you to take control of each day and move toward living the life of your dreams.

My objective in writing this book is *to help you help yourself*: to connect you to the most accurate central processing unit there is—you! To do this, I will provide you with a step-by-step approach to a method—complete with exercises—which I have labeled "the 12 Disciplines." Living the lifestyle of your choice requires a conscious effort to master the 12 Disciplines, but it's a straightforward course of action, and it's available to everyone.

In most organizations, management devotes enormous energy to setting work objectives and conducting performance reviews for individual employees. Corporations go through this time-consuming and costly exercise to ensure the most favorable results for their firm. In professions such as sales, considerable time is spent discovering and understanding the needs of clients in order to provide a recommended action plan.

In contrast, how much time and energy do you expend discovering your own needs and desires, and then consciously setting objectives, developing action plans with measurable performance standards, and finally reviewing your own performance? By engaging in such an exercise, you will be doing something about your life. You will be going to work *on yourself*, for yourself.

What's different about this book? First of all, this book is not about getting you high for a day or two. It is a self-discovery companion and planning guide that will make a significant difference in your life. It is based on adult learning principles and the adage that "I could give you a fish and feed you for a day, or I can teach you how to fish and feed you for life." My intention is the latter, to provide you with the tools to help you find and lead the life you crave.

To benefit from this book will require some discipline on your part as you learn about self-motivation and personal leadership. You must complete each exercise as it appears. As you complete them you will start to realize that only you can make the difference in your life. By doing the exercises, you are going through a self-discovery process. As you discover, you take ownership, and that is what makes the difference. Because it is your idea, you own it and you are more committed to making it happen.

You now have in your hands the ideas and tools, combined with an internationally proven adult learning process, for you to make the difference in your life. The choice is yours, but it *will* take discipline.

This book is divided into two parts. Part I is a process of self-discovery and self-understanding. Once your concept of success is defined and you know your personal rights, you can make the decisions needed to take control of your life. Meanwhile, you will learn about yourself, what you want out of life, and how you want to be remembered.

In Part II, taking all the elements of Part I into consideration, you will crystallize your dreams into an action plan. This book's techniques and tools will guide you through the process. You just have to do the work and put your plan into action.

The process will be driven by you and it is thought-provoking work. I have tried to make it as easy as I could for you by sharing some personal life experiences and examples. However, if you complete each exercise as it appears, and if you monitor and measure your progress every month, I promise you that you will be rewarded far beyond your expectations.

Over the years I have come to realize that I enjoy helping people. This is part of what led me to become a self-motivation speaker and sales trainer. Speakers and authors like Anthony Robbins, Brian Tracy, Mark Victor Hansen, Zig Ziglar, Tom Hopkins, Stephen Covey, Og Mandino, Napoleon Hill and Norman Vincent Peale have inspired me over the last 25 years and have helped me get to where I am today. Using my own life experiences as a guide, I have consolidated the best of what they and others have offered to produce this practical approach to lifestyle change.

As a teenager, I didn't know what I wanted to do or where I wanted to go. My mind was cluttered with conflicting ideas from school, religion, family and friends. I didn't even know who I really was. All I knew was what others told me about myself. My whole life was driven by others.

When I turned 20, I began to explore the powers of the mind and how attitude plays a significant role in everything. I became obsessed with it. Everything I read was about attitude, motivation and goal setting. I became so focused in this area that I ignored the world around me. I was so busy understanding the mind and its capabilities that I couldn't find the time to pay attention to daily news events. I hope to impart to you the importance of leading a healthy and well-balanced life while at the same time staying focused on your goals.

In order to take full advantage of this book, and your life, highlight your favorite passages and write down your thoughts. Start now by writing your name in the space provided at the front of the book. Complete all the exercises in the order that they occur, and add your thoughts in the space provided at the end of each chapter. Keep this as your personal journal and reference book. If you need more space, order the *Online for Life* workbook (ordering information is located at the back of this book).

You will learn a lot about yourself. By taking your time, thinking things out and writing down your thoughts, you will immediately begin to reap rewards.

Your self-image, self-respect, self-esteem, and the manner in which you portray yourself to the world will improve. You will lead yourself to the life of your choice. Why? Because nobody else will. You are the only person responsible and accountable for you.

One final note: before moving on from one discipline to the next, recognize and reward yourself by celebrating the completion of all the exercises in that discipline.

Now let's move on to Part I and discover what success, attitude and motivation are all about. Have fun!

Part I

⌒

Understanding Success, Attitude, Motivation and That Most Important Person—You

"All of your dreams
can come true—if you
have the courage to
pursue them."

Walt Disney

To Start

Success is based on imagination, plus ambition and the will.

Thomas A. Edison

What does success mean to you? This can be a difficult question because we often look to others as examples. We see the Smiths down the street with a beautiful home, a swimming pool and a new car. By the looks of things, we might consider the Smiths successful, since most people tend to base success on material possessions. But are they, or is it just a front to try to impress the neighbors? For all we know, they could hate what they are doing, they could be heavily in debt and not very happy. So why do we judge people by their external appearances and material possessions and compare ourselves with their apparent success? Is *that* what success is all about?

Success means different things to different people. The reality is, success means whatever you want it to mean for you. Don't compare yourself with others and what they think success means. Believe it or not, you are already successful in many different ways. You just haven't taken the time to realize it yet. I am sure you've succeeded in accomplishing many of the things

you desired in life—learning to ride a bike, learning to read and write, graduating, buying a car or a home, finding the right person and getting married, having children, and so on. These are all desires, or goals, that you have accomplished. You have succeeded so far in your life, haven't you?

Look back again at the two different ways we have looked at success. In the first paragraph we looked at success from an external point of view—we compared ourselves to others. In the second paragraph we considered success from an internal point of view—a view of our desires in life—and they don't have to concern money, power or material things. Your desire could be for a certain lifestyle, education, career, marriage or anything you want to have, be or do.

Success is the progressive accomplishment of a worthy goal or idea. If there is something you want to have, be or do, and you move forward to accomplishing that desire, you succeed. Success is not just about material things, it's about you. Success is not about how society sees you, it's about how you see yourself.

How you see yourself is what Part I is all about. It is an *inside-out* approach to success. You have to know yourself and your personal motivators if you want to travel the road of personal success and happiness.

How do you see yourself? It is important at this stage that you start by recognizing your successes. Take a few moments now and list some of them.

Some of my successes to date include:

6 ultra-successful RMT practices

BSc degree. Premed. 1-yr BC RMT upgrade. Masters' level Anat.
2.5 yrs of successful marriage.

_____

_____

_____

Obviously, you have achieved a great deal in life through dedication, hard work and discipline. Now let's pretend, for the next couple of minutes, that nothing is impossible and that you can have, be or do anything you want in life. What would that be?

Be as descriptive as possible.

Continuously successful, challenging / relaxing life doing
doing meaningful work
Owning a house it don't explain h nearly mtrs for retreat
Writing + teaching part time, have an ass't to org + promote this
w/ kick-ass partner + her child, spiritual sexual connection.
Appreciated / Appreciating friends. Fun time. (fr
Great feeling of accomplishment, success, happiness. Great attitude.
Abundance. Lotsa money.

Now take a look at what you wrote. Is this what you really want? Will it make you happier? Do you have the desire to go out and get it? What if it became reality? How would you feel? Can you see yourself already there? Can you hear the sounds, and the things being said about you? If you have the desire and if you can feel it, see it and hear it, you are well on your way to being there.

Why? Because of your attitude. It is your attitude that will make the biggest difference in your life. Your past and present are a result of your past attitude. However, your present attitude will determine your future. The greatest thing about attitude is that it is 100 percent under your control.

> *Whether you think you can, or you think you can't, you're absolutely right.*
>
> Henry Ford

Your attitude is created by your beliefs. Your beliefs were developed in your past. It may be time to re-evaluate them. Your present-day beliefs determine your attitude. It is your attitude that determines how you feel. How you feel determines how you act, and how you act determines your results in the realization of your dream.

How you see yourself, your self-worth, your self-esteem and your self-confidence is all part of your attitude. How others see you, or perceive you, can influence your attitude, as it has in the past. That is external influence. If you accept that influence, whether it be positive or negative, you will let it affect you internally. However, if you become aware of those external influences and decide to lead from within, you start to take control of your attitude.

Your attitude is you and what you believe your future to be.
Do you have a desire for you and your future?   YES.

Attitude

Rate yourself on a scale from 1 to 10 on how you feel about your attitude.

Poor ——————————————— *Excellent*

1 2 3 4 5 6 7 8 9 10

*I'm here currently —
lowest to myself - esteem/attitude.*   *usually, this my identified
self attitude*

Why did you rate yourself like that?
Rejection from Erin (real + perceived).

What must you do to be a 10?
① Get back on my road to purpose.
② Realize my successes. Rebuild confidence.

— envision success

The 12 Disciplines for Living Your Dreams

The basic principles of success are (1) inspiration to action—self-motivation; (2) know-how; (3) activity knowledge.

W. Clement Stone

It is desire and the envisaging of success that creates self-motivation. When you can see, feel and hear the outcome of your desire, you create the belief that it will happen. These expectations motivate you toward those images of success.

Motivation is a desire held in the expectation that it will be accomplished. It all starts with desire—having a burning passion for something. Without desire, you cannot be motivated. Once the desire has set in, you must see, hear and feel your dream—be able to visualize it in detail *as if it already exists*. This is the only true form of motivation because it comes from inside you.

Motivation is *a motive for action*. We are motivated toward images of success, which we expect to provide us with pleasure and gain. At the same time, we are motivated to avoid failure, pain and loss. If we keep images of success, pleasure and gain in our mind, we will be motivated toward them. However, if we keep images of failure, pain and loss foremost in our mind, we will be motivated merely to stay away from them, or just not motivated at all.

Unfortunately, so many people waste their time on the latter, and are not self-motivated at all. They rely on external motivators, like lottery tickets and incentives. These many forms of external motivators have a problem—their effect doesn't last. As soon as you acquire an incentive, you'll want a bigger and better one. As soon as you face up to a threat, the threat will no longer stop you. The only true form of motivation comes from you, for you.

Motivation is the ability to see, in the present, a projection of the future that you want for yourself. In the exercise that you just completed, you defined a goal and you've seen, heard and felt its accomplishment. But the process doesn't end there. You have to take your desire and put it into motion by developing a plan for its achievement. Move steadily towards that vision day by day. We will discuss this in Part II: Creating Your Future, One Step at a Time.

Now that we have an understanding of success, attitude and motivation from an internal source—you—let's continue with Part I. In the following disciplines you will review your rights, make a decision, and start to take control of your life. You will get to know yourself and what you want out of life, and you will define how you want to be remembered. This part involves serious soul-searching. Take your time, think things over, sleep on them and continue the next day. You can always add to your lists. This is a very important part and you must complete it fully before moving on.

I hope that this brief introduction has prepared you to tackle the 12 Disciplines. Let's get started with Discipline # 1: Know Your Rights.

Discipline #1
Know Your Rights ⌒

Truth will always be truth, regardless of lack of understanding, disbelief or ignorance.

W. Clement Stone

As human beings we have many rights, and there are at least ten rights that I think you need to be aware of. They are the rights to our success. All of them are disciplines within themselves and should be mastered. It is important for you to first understand your rights before you truly begin your journey to mastering self-motivation and personal leadership. You will also find these rights to be a great inspiration.

1. **You have the right to your dreams, desires and expectations.**
   Do you agree? [✓] yes [ ] no. If no, why?

   _____

   _____

Nothing happens unless first a dream.

Carl Sandburg

Can you imagine what life would be like if we could not dream? What would the world look like? Where would we be today? It all starts with a dream.

Our dreams become our desires. It is that burning desire, combined with the belief that you can do it, that provides you with your motivation to make your dream a reality. And when you release that passion inside of you to accomplish your dream, nothing will stand in your way.

Think back to a dream or a desire you once had. It could have been to graduate, to travel to an exotic destination, to acquire a particular item, to be a certain type of person or to find a spouse, a home or a certain type of friend or acquaintance. Did you not live that dream?

Like you, I too have lived many dreams. I could tell you about many occasions where my dreams have become reality. For example, I can remember when I was in my early twenties, I wanted to own my own home. I didn't want to pay rent, because I saw that money just flying out of the window—I got no return other than shelter. My soon-to-be-wife and I dreamed of owning our own home in the Gatineau Hills. We had a strong desire. We believed we could do it, even though we were told we couldn't. Having both graduated and started our first jobs, we expected it to be feasible. We expected it to happen. We had high expectations. Few things come easily, as you will see in the tenth right. Our dream, our desire and our persistence to win were tested. Weren't yours?

2. **You have the right to have what you want.**

   Do you agree? [ ] yes [ ] no. If no, why?

   _____

   _____

   Be what you are, and become what you are capable of becoming.

   Robert Louis Stevenson

The 12 Disciplines for Living Your Dreams

We wanted a house in the Gatineau Hills, just outside of Ottawa, Canada's capital city. We made an offer on one. We wanted it, but we didn't get it. We were too young, not in our jobs long enough, and didn't have enough money for a deposit. All the external forces told me it was not possible. Internally, I knew it was possible. It was my right to have what I wanted.

After being rejected, we realized that we had to get creative. We got a personal loan and bought a building lot.

When we said we were going to build a home, everyone asked, "What do you know about building? You've never even held a hammer." My response was, "So, I'll learn. Building a house is not rocket science." All the external forces were telling me, "You can't have it, you can't do it, it's impossible." But I believed in myself and I didn't let those negative forces stop me from living my dream.

Doesn't this happen to us often? When we want to have something, the external forces are there to tell us differently. We could fall into the trap, forget the whole stupid idea, and go on with our mediocre lives. Yet, if we believe enough in ourselves and in our dreams, if we persist and expect to succeed, things have a way of working out.

We bought the building lot in the winter, and when summer came we still did not feel comfortable about approaching the bank for financing. Although we had had another six months working in our jobs, we had that personal loan to deal with and no other funds. We were about ready to agree that it couldn't be done. Then, something happened. It was like a reward for believing in our dream.

The best man at our wedding, John, proudly announced he had just received a $10,000 bonus for exceeding his sales results in the last year. After congratulating him and celebrating the occasion, I had a creative thought. I said, "John, you never did give us a wedding gift." He replied, "I'm not giving you $10,000." "That's not what I had in mind," I said. "How about giving me an interest-free loan for 30 days? At the end of 30 days, or earlier, you get it back." John agreed. It saved him spending any money or effort on a wedding gift. And it provided us with the funds to start building our home.

Throughout this experience we were constantly being tested on our dream, our desire, and our belief in ourselves. It would have been so easy to give up, to let the external forces win. Fortunately, I had already discovered the powers of the mind and realized that things happen from the inside out, not from the outside in.

3. **You have the right to like yourself as you are.**
    Do you agree? [ ] yes [ ] no. If no, why?

    _____

    _____

> *Nothing splendid has ever been achieved except by those who dared believe that something inside of them was superior to circumstances.*
>
> Bruce Barton

Most of us go through life accepting too many external comments that lead us to believe that we are not good enough, attractive enough, strong enough, experienced enough, and the list goes on. Until we realize who we really are, we can fall into these traps and stay there.

In our younger years we picked up a lot of baggage. Some of it was good and some of it was not so good. Most of the time, as children, we believed what we were told. Many people received positive reinforcement, while others received negative comments. Anyone that was overweight, underweight, tall or short, handicapped or different, knows what I am talking about. The comments that we accepted as truth became part of us and led us to liking ourselves, or disliking ourselves, as we are.

We also compared ourselves to others and wished we had the looks, size, shape or qualities of someone else. Many times in our lives we may not have liked ourselves as we are, mostly because of external influences or comments. While at other times, in certain environments, we liked ourselves as we are either because of internal beliefs or external influences and comments.

For example, as a young boy, my mother, aunts and grandmother would always grab my cheek and tell me how cute and how special I was because I had dimples. When I started going to school the girls told me I was cute. By the time I was ten, I believed I was cute.

By the time I became a teenager, life took a turn on me. Those cute dimples turned into ugly pimples. What do you think society told me then? Right, I was ugly. And the more times I would look into the mirror, the more I agreed with them. I was ugly.

I became extremely shy. I avoided people, and avoided going out. I would hear people saying how unattractive I was, and talking about it behind my back. I even found it difficult to look at myself in the mirror. I basically hid and lost five years of my life. I did not like myself as I was.

Finally, someone approached me and told me about a girl who wanted to go to the graduation dance with me. It took me three weeks and a lot of courage to ask her. Shortly afterwards, my wife-to-be looked beyond what she saw on the outside because the acne didn't matter to her. She gave me the gift of inner strength.

It was that newly found inner strength that caused me to wake up one day and look into the mirror *again*. As I looked into the mirror, I came to a great realization. Everyone has an outer shelter—skin—that they can hide behind. But it is what is behind that skin that really matters. Yes, I had acne, but I came to the conclusion that I liked the guy inside. As I realized this, I started to emerge from my shell. From that point on I decided to take control of my life and lead my life from the inside out, as opposed to the outside in. In fact, it was this inside-out approach that gave me the courage to eventually become a profession-al speaker.

Since then, I've liked myself as I am. I know myself, my values, my strengths and weaknesses, my dreams and desires.

4. **You have the right to change.**

Do you agree? [ ] yes [ ] no. If no, why?

_____

_____

> *It is possible, at any time, to change one's career and goals and way of life.*
>
> Paul Gauguin

This is a special power that we have. We can change a multitude of things in our lives simply by making a single decision and committing to it. Take a moment and think about some of the things you want to change in your life. Have you done an attitude check recently? What are your first thoughts on a rainy morning? How do you treat others? What is your out-look on life?

As a teenager, I changed myself as I changed schools. I consciously changed my name from Bobby to Bob. I changed shy Bobby into outgo-ing Bob. Later in my teenage years, as I learned about the powers of the mind, I changed my outlook on life from external to internal. It became important for me to realize my own dreams.

When I started my career I changed my language to be more busi-nesslike. As I changed jobs and acquired more responsibility, I improved my work habits. When I got married I changed, as I had children I changed, and when I went into business for myself I changed.

We are constantly changing. What we must keep in mind, though, is that we do not always change for the right reasons. We let circumstances change us. But changes should be internally driven, not circumstance driven. Look inside and consciously choose the changes you want to make in your life.

When we make a decision to do something, we take a risk. It takes courage to change, because change is not always successful. And this is where many people give in.

5. **You have the right to fail.**

Do you agree? [ ] yes [ ] no. If no, why?

_____

_____

Failure is the opportunity to begin again more intelligently.

Henry Ford

When society realizes the good that comes out of failure, and recognizes people for trying, the world will be better for it. All success comes from failure. No one in the world has succeeded without first trying, failing, learning, making changes, and moving on. Always remember that you have the right to fail; you no longer have to make excuses for your failed attempts. Instead, reflect on that failure and learn from it. That experience will provide you with better judgment for the future, and will eventually lead you to success.

Success is based on good judgment. Good judgment comes from experience. And how does one get experience? Sometimes we have to fail often to succeed once. But that fear of failure stops us from even trying. That is one of the reasons we procrastinate. We think about it too much. If you just do it and fail, what is the worst thing that can happen? You will learn a lesson. If you really want to succeed, you may have to double your failure rate.

After losing five years of my life hiding as a teenager with acne, I realized I had some catching up to do. I developed a "do it now" attitude. I no longer thought endlessly about things because I realized that the longer I thought about doing something, the longer I would hesitate before doing it; or, I might not do it at all. I put procrastination behind me and started to just do things without thinking, realizing that the worst that could happen is that I would learn something.

Failure is part of my daily life. I don't always take the time to think things out. I am a doer; I learn and move forward by doing. This gives me lots of opportunities to fail, and to be criticized. I have experienced so much failure in my life that I am now wise because of it.

I believe that both failure and success are part of life's balance. The more you try, the more you fail, *and* the more you succeed. If you don't try, you'll neither fail nor succeed.

Failure is not easy to accept. You need to be able to see the good behind every experience in life. Rather than criticizing yourself or others for failure, recognize the things that were done right, the effort of trying, and the lessons learned. So, what is stopping you from moving forward?

6. **You have the right to be imperfect.**

   Do you agree? [ ] yes [ ] no. If no, why?

   _____

   _____

> *To talk about the need for perfection in man is to talk about the need for another species. The essence of man is imperfection.*
>
> Norman Cousins

Society has put a lot of pressure on us to perform, and imperfection, like failure, is not popular. But we have to understand that nobody is perfect.

We could strive for the goal of perfection, but is it realistic? We can only do our best. We all have imperfections: physical, mental or spiritual. Realize this in others, too, and treat them with respect.

Imagine if we were all perfect. What kind of world would that be? There would be no opportunities, no challenges; failure would not exist. Would we learn anything? Do you think we would be happier? I don't think so. Thank God for the differences and imperfections in each of us— and our great opportunities to learn.

Each of us has strengths and weaknesses. If we can find people whose strengths are our weaknesses, and our strengths are their weaknesses, we can form an effective team. Only through others can we truly increase our state of perfection.

Remember that you have the right to be imperfect, and so do others. But we also can choose to do, or not to do, something about it.

7. **You have the right to choose.**

Do you agree? [ ] yes [ ] no. If no, why?

_____

_____

> *As human beings, we are endowed with freedom of choice and we cannot shuffle off our responsibility upon the shoulders of God or nature. We must shoulder it ourselves. It is up to us.*
>
> Arnold J. Toynbee

This is our greatest gift. We can choose our dreams: to be what we want, go where we want, do what we want, have what we want, and react to circumstances in the way we want.

Each day we make choices, from the moment we wake up to the time we fall asleep. There are the obvious choices: what to eat, wear and do that day. There are also the not-so-obvious choices: our thoughts, our attitudes, and our behaviors. These options are also under our full control.

It all begins with the choices in our thoughts. Our whole thought process is under our full control. We can choose to think of things in a positive light or in a negative light. We can call the glass half empty or half full. We can choose to strive for accomplishment or we can worry and expect fear and failure. We can accept that a problem controls us, or we can choose to see ourselves in control, and look for the opportunity hidden behind the circumstances. It's up to us.

We can choose to accept or reject criticism and negativity. We can also choose to accept positive strokes or reject them. We have control over our thoughts. Our thoughts control our destiny. Our choice to control, or not control, our thoughts will make the difference in our attitudes and behaviors.

Our thoughts are influenced by many factors. We were conditioned by our parents, school, family and friends. Now as adults, our environment still conditions us but we can distinguish and choose between good and bad, truth and fiction, if we take the time. We are a product of our environment, and we must be aware of what that has done to our thought process. We have to make choices about our thoughts in order to take control of them.

I remember when I became aware of my right to choose. It made a big difference in me. I started to look at things differently—to consider the options available. I realized that I could do anything I chose to, as long as I was aware and in control of my self-talk, my thoughts and my actions.

You have so many choices to make in life. I encourage you to be aware of the choices in your thought process, where it all begins. A desire is a thought. It is followed by choices—choices that will lead you to decisions. Indecision leads to doubt; combined, they produce fear that paralyzes us. Consider your choices, and make a decision to commit to your choice. Then it is up to you to make that choice work.

It's your life and it is up to you how you live it. Your desires and aspirations, or your limitations and fears, are all your choice. If you are not sure of your choices, ask!

8. **You have the right to ask.**
   Do you agree? [ ] yes [ ] no. If no, why?

   _____

   _____

> *Ask and it shall be given you; seek and ye shall find;*
> *knock and it shall be opened unto you. For every one that*
> *asketh receiveth; and he that seeketh, findeth; and to him*
> *that knocketh it shall be opened.*
>
> Luke 11:9-10

If we don't ask for something, how are we ever going to get it? By simply not asking, the answer is automatically a no. But is that not the reason why we don't ask? We don't want to be rejected. Understand what was said above – you don't ask, you don't get. When you do ask, do you not increase your chances of getting a yes? You already know that the worst answer you can get is a no. Therefore, why not ask and increase your chances of getting a yes. Make it a habit to ask, but be careful what you ask for because you may get it!

Imagine the salesperson who doesn't ask questions to understand the prospect's needs or ask for the order. Picture the person who doesn't ask for the promotion; the person who doesn't ask for a hand in marriage. Do they get what they want? Don't ever be shy to ask. What is the worst response you can get? "No." So, what have you lost? You can't lose something you never had. Now, imagine you ask the same question and the answer is yes, just for asking. How much further ahead would you be now?

If I hadn't asked my wife Joan to go to the high school graduation with me I may never have found that wonderful and loving partner. If I hadn't asked my friend John for a loan, we may not have been able to build our first home, nor been able to live in our dream home of today. If I hadn't asked for guidance, I likely wouldn't have received it. And if I hadn't asked myself what I wanted out of life, I doubt I'd be where I (happily) am today.

Ask of yourself, ask of others, and ask often. Don't ever be shy to ask. If you don't ask, you don't get.

Indeed, the *more* you ask, the more you get. If you need help, if you want a promotion, if you want a referral, if you do not understand something, if you want more out of life, what must you do? Ask! You do have the right to ask! Make it a habit to ask. Asking can help you to choose how to use your time and energy most effectively.

9. **You have the right to decide how you will use your time and energy.**
   Do you agree? [ ] yes [ ] no. If no, why?

   _____

   _____

> *The whole secret of freedom from anxiety over not having enough time lies not in working more hours, but in the proper planning of the hours.*
>
> Frank Bettger

Maybe you have a job and other responsibilities where there are expectations of you. But who decided to take on these responsibilities? I understand. You needed a job and you had no choice. I've been there. But think about this: is what you are doing bringing you closer to the realization of your dreams? If so, great! If not, maybe you should reconsider how you are using your time and energy. You have the right to decide how much effort you invest toward achieving your goals.

I once worked for a large corporation that had a performance review process. Employees and their supervisors set objectives for the year and reviewed them quarterly. Individuals spent a lot of time and energy on the reviews and appraisals—up to five days a year. This was a great form of discipline, and worth the effort because feedback improves job performance.

But whose dreams are we being appraised on? Is that appraisal, or feedback, an internal or an external process? By the way, who is the most important person in the world? How much time and energy do we provide directly to that person and his or her dreams?

Similarly, salespeople claim to spend their time qualifying and understanding the needs of prospects. But I wonder how many of them have taken the time to qualify themselves and understand the needs of the person they see in the mirror.

So, what about a personal performance review of your life expectations?

How many jobs will you go through to find career happiness? How much time and energy do you put into looking in the mirror to discover the needs and desires of the person you see there? Have you set out an annual or lifetime plan of action for that person? Are you checking on his or her performance? Where should you be spending your time and energy? Think about it. You know who the most important person in the world is and you have the right to decide how you will use your time and energy.

10. **You have the right to lunch when you pay for it; there is no free lunch.**

Do you agree? [ ] yes [ ] no. If no, why?

_____

_____

> *The people who get on in this world are the people who get up and look for the circumstances they want, and, if they can't find them, make them.*
>
> George Bernard Shaw

Nothing in life is free, nor will it get delivered to you on a silver platter. You have to work for what you want, and what you put out is what you will get. Everything happens in direct proportion to the effort you expend. You can have and do what you want and be who you want to be, but you have to make it happen.

Are you ready to start to make it happen? _____

The rest of this book will help you help yourself to make it happen.

We have the right(s) to so much. What's holding you back?

Summary ⌒

Discipline # 1: Know Your Rights

1. You have the right to your dreams, desires and expectations.
2. You have the right to have what you want.
3. You have the right to like yourself as you are.
4. You have the right to change.
5. You have the right to fail.
6. You have the right to be imperfect.
7. You have the right to choose.
8. You have the right to ask.
9. You have the right to decide how you will use your time and energy.
10. You have the right to lunch when you pay for it; there is no free lunch.

Thought space

Take an inside-out way of life. (And I do!) My relationships, belongings, job do not necessarily reflect my inner self.

_____
_____
_____
_____
_____
_____
_____
_____
_____
_____
_____
_____
_____
_____
_____
_____
_____
_____
_____

Discipline #2
Make a Decision

It's your decisions, and not your conditions, that shape your destiny.

Anthony Robbins

This could be a turning point for you. You have the right to decide how you want to live your life. People who have lived full lives haven't done so by accident. They've made a conscious decision sometime during their life that they were going to accomplish something and live the life of their choice.

You too can live the life of your choice. You could live the life of someone else's choice, or you may settle for a combination of your desires and someone else's. Also, you could decide not to make a decision at all. The point is that no one else is going to make that decision for you—you must make it for yourself. Until you make that decision, you will drift aimlessly through life, directed by circumstances and external factors instead of shaping your own future. Whichever way you decide, make the effort to stick to that choice.

There will be tough times when you question your decisions, but that will only test your commitment. When you make a decision to go after your dreams, expect resistance from some people. They will feel uncomfortable because they have given up on their own dreams. Be determined and ready to face resistance, to climb over those obstacles. You must persist. Success will come little by little, as you do things each day. Are you ready to commit yourself to the life of your choice?

When I first met Andrij, a student who worked for me one summer, I asked him what he wanted to accomplish during that work period. His answer was, "I don't know." I persisted, "Well, what do you want to accomplish next year?" "I don't know." I asked, "What do you want out of life?" Again he replied, "I don't know." Is this the way you want to live your life—aimlessly?

When I was a teenager, I was no different. I wanted to be a success. But, what was success? It was whatever others told me it was. It was to have a job, a wife, family, home, automobile and money. But what did I want? Did I want to live the life society laid out for me, or the one that was 'truly' me? When I realized that my life was my choice, and I was the only one responsible for it, I took full advantage of my decision-making capabilities. I decided to live the life of my choice, of my dreams, to the best of my capability.

If you don't make a choice, you are just passing through and leaving life to chance. Don't settle for circumstances or chance. Life is not about chance, it's about choice! You have the freedom to choose the life you want. The first step is to decide that you are going to live the life of your choice.

Do you avoid making decisions? If you said yes, you are not alone. Many of us freeze when faced with decisions, even small ones. We're afraid of making the wrong choice.

> *Believing in your own ideas, abilities, and decision-making capabilities is the first step to achieving success in life.*
>
> Dr. Wayne W. Dyer

If you're one of those people who hate to make decisions, you can be sure of one thing. This inability to make decisions can stop you dead in your tracks and hinder you on the road to success. You end up waiting for things to happen instead of making them happen. You doubt your commitments and you turn away from your dreams, the dreams you know could be achieved. The result is tremendous unhappiness, multiple failures and lost opportunities, deep frustration, endless procrastination and abiding hopelessness.

There is something you can do about this. You can gain confidence in your ability to make decisions and make the process easier and more successful. We have a range of options to choose from when we must make a decision. We discard an option when we withdraw ourselves from it. An option becomes a decision when we invest ourselves in it.

What makes a decision work? It is almost always the decision maker, and not the choice, that makes it work. Failure is proportional to lack of dedicated commitment. Choices are good only if we *make* them good.

The first step of a successful decision is to make that decision. The act of making a decision is almost always more important than the substance of the decision itself. Conversely, making no choice—indecision—invalidates all options because it paralyzes us. But the more we make decisions, the more natural the process becomes.

Consider your options, think about your choices, observe your feelings—and make a decision about your life. Commit to that decision in every way possible; make it work.

To live the life of your choice you will have to be internally driven. You will need to take an inside-out approach to life. You will need to be consciously aware of what is being said or happening around you and decide if you want to be part of that external environment. If not, you must find or create the environment that is conducive to who you want to be and where you want to go. We are all products of our environment.

This reminds me of when I was just starting out as a professional speaker. The only professional speakers' association in Canada at that time was in Toronto. I wanted to become a product of that sort of environment. I became a member but found it too far to go for evening meetings, so I asked if I could create a chapter in Ottawa. There was no such environment in Ottawa, so I decided to create one. One that would assist me, and others, in the realization of our dreams. It wasn't long after, that the Ottawa Chapter of the Canadian Association of Professional Speakers was founded. Why? Because I knew what I wanted, created a plan and made it happen.

There are three types of people in this world:

1. There are those who just don't know or can't decide—Andrij, my summer student, for example. He didn't know what he wanted or where he was going. He didn't know that he had a choice. He was wandering around without focus, hoping that circumstances would take care of him.

2. There are those who wish and dream, but do nothing about it. These are the type of people who depend on a winning lottery ticket. You've heard them: "If I won a million dollars I would..." They expect something for nothing and they don't realize there is a price to pay for everything in life—they have to make an effort.

3. There are those who know what they want, plan for it, and go out and get it. These are the people others usually call lucky. But these people had a dream, created a plan, implemented it, persisted, and maybe even failed along the way, until they got what they wanted.

The 12 Disciplines for Living Your Dreams

Which type are you now? [ ] Type 1   [ ] Type 2   [ ] Type 3

Which type do you want to be? [ ] Type 1   [ ] Type 2   [ ] Type 3

You just made a decision. If you didn't, go back and make that decision now, as you will soon have to make more decisions. If you decided you wanted to be a type 1 or type 2, nothing will change. You will remain externally driven and a product of your environment. If you decided that you want to be a type 3, you have taken your first step towards personal leadership. You have decided to live the life of your dreams, to identify what you want, plan for it and make it happen. This is an everlasting, internally driven process.

The first step to internal (self-) motivation is to make decisions—to do something about your life—not just accept what comes along. You will need discipline and courage, determination and persistence, imagination, a positive attitude, a strong belief in yourself, and faith that nothing is impossible. This book will provide you with the direction and exercises to get you where you've never been before. You will drown your greatest fears, you will live your greatest moments, and you will fulfill your dreams.

If you prefer to accept life as it comes, don't bother reading on. You will be wasting your time. This book is dedicated to those who are prepared to pay the price of hard work and determination in order to take control of their lives and their destination.

Take the time now to think about your options. Think about the obstacles, the work involved, and the possible outcomes. You could decide to live a life of no change, effort or decision; or you could decide to take action and live the life of your choice. Which will it be?

Online for Life

My decision is to:

_____

_____

_____

_____

_____

If you decided to take action and live the life of your choice, please sign below as a form of commitment to yourself. You are choosing to do whatever it takes to make your decision work, a decision that will require effort, determination and perseverance. Are you ready to complete all the exercises in this book? Are you truly committed? If so, sign now!

Signature: _____

Date: _____

Summary ⌒

Discipline # 2: Make a Decision

Which will it be? Make a decision to do something about your life and live the life of your dreams **or** to accept life as it comes.

The first step in self-motivation is to make the decision to do something about your life, not just accept life as it happens.

It is almost always the decision maker, and not the choice, that makes the decision work.

The first part of the successful decision is to make that decision. The act of making a decision is almost always more important than the substance of the decision itself. Conversely, making no choice—indecision—invalidates all options because it paralyzes you.

The more we make decisions, the more natural the process becomes.

There are three types of people in this world:
1. Those who don't know or can't decide on what they want;
2. Those who wish and dream and do nothing about it;
3. Those who know what they want, plan for it, and go out and get it.

Thought space

_____

_____

_____

_____

_____

_____

_____

Online for Life

Discipline #3
Take Control of Your Life

Habits are powerful factors in our lives. Because they are consistent, often unconscious patterns, they constantly, daily, express our character and produce our effectiveness...or ineffectiveness.

Stephen R. Covey

There are things in life that we cannot control, and things that are under our full control. One of the first things we must do is get into the habit of distinguishing which is which. Then we can start to take control of our lives and our destiny.

Each day we go out into the world where we are faced with the many external influences that are not part of ourselves, not under our control, and that cause us to react. Influences like the weather, the news, the traffic, the crowds of people or the lack of people, and the comments we hear. When you wake up to a rainy day, versus a sunny day, do you see things differently? When you get caught in traffic, how do you react? When faced with an obstacle, or failure, what do you do?

How we react is under our full control. We have that freedom of choice.

We can react as favorably to a rainy day as we would to a sunny day, appreciating what good the rain does, or we can complain about the clouds. When we get caught in traffic we can get upset, which does us no good because we cannot control the traffic, or we can use the time to visualize our dreams. When we face an obstacle we can be discouraged and even quit, or we can seek out the hidden opportunity, knowing that at least we will learn from the experience.

A state of mind cannot be purchased, it must be created. Your states of mind are your thoughts. You can improve the quality of your life by managing your thoughts, by reframing them so that they empower rather than depress you. As an adult, you have absolute control over your own thoughts. Your thoughts control your attitude and determine how you react to situations. Your thoughts are you!

Because you have the ability to control your own state of mind, you can overcome habits and even fears. You have the capability and the right to accept or reject your thoughts. It's called willpower.

If you fail to control your own mind, how can you control anything else? Control your thoughts or your thoughts will control you. There is no halfway compromise. Mind control is a result of self-discipline and habit. Keep your mind busy with a definite purpose backed by a definite plan.

Our thought process and our reactions make the difference in our lives. To take control of our lives we must first identify the things we have no control over versus the things we do have control over.

Things I have no control over include:

_____

_____

_____

_____

_____

Write them down. Think of the things that upset you. Go beyond the weather, traffic, noise, flight delays or waiting on people. List as many things as possible.

Things I do have control over include:

_____

_____

_____

_____

_____

Any difference between the two? Did you notice that the things that are not under your control are external to you, while the things under your control are internal? This is the source of the only true form of motivation.

Start by taking control of the things that are under your control. Take a close look at your beliefs and re-evaluate them. You are now an adult and can distinguish between what is real and what is not. Some of it is negative baggage you picked up along the way, perhaps as a child.

You may have been told something that you accepted as the truth at the time and it became part of your belief system. That belief may have stopped you from doing the things you enjoy or want to do.

For example, when I was a teenager, I enjoyed dancing. I thought I was a good dancer until I was told differently. I can clearly remember being teased by my brother and friends. Teased to the point where, until recently, I avoided dancing at any cost. Yet, my wife's greatest pleasure is dancing.

Obviously, those negative comments had a big impact on my life, and my wife's satisfaction. The comments were external to me, but back then I chose to internalize them and make them part of me. I had let something that was not under my control—what others said about me—influence me. Years later, I came to realize that how I reacted to their comments was under my control. Because I have taken the time to think and become aware of this belief, I have decided to rid myself of that baggage. I want to dance, and I want to dance my wife off her feet!

Similarly, many years ago I internalized the belief that to succeed I must go the extra mile. The problem I have is identifying where that mile ends, as moderation is not one of my strengths. This is a belief that I fully support. But, at what cost? Recently, I've made the effort to re-evaluate this belief, in search of a degree of moderation and a balanced lifestyle.

You probably have similar baggage. Your assignment is to identify your inappropriate beliefs, in the space provided below, so you can later create a plan to replace them with appropriate beliefs.

Inappropriate beliefs:

_____

_____

_____

_____

_____

_____

_____

Your beliefs drive your attitude. Your attitude drives everything! Change your beliefs and you change your attitude. What is your attitude like on a rainy day when you have outdoor plans or on a beautiful sunny day when you have to go to work? Do you make the best of it or do you complain about it?

Your attitude is a direct reflection of your beliefs. Your attitude determines how you feel. It is how you feel that determines how you act. How you act, determines your results. All of which are under your control. Are they not?

The 12 Disciplines for Living Your Dreams

Let's take a look at your attitude. Do you have an attitude of gratitude? What is your attitude towards yourself? Your attitudes are your thoughts. Do you talk to yourself? What do you say? Is it positive or negative? Are you even aware of what you are saying?

Research says that up to 70 percent of our self-talk is negative and that it takes 11 positive statements to reverse one negative thought. That's a lot of work. Your first challenge is to become aware of what you are saying and what you are thinking, as our thoughts of today dictate the reality of our tomorrow.

I can remember when I was in my twenties working as a sales representative for a major oil company and doing a lot of driving. I drove so much that I could not help but think about the mileage I was doing. I would say to myself that I was increasing my chances of having a car accident because I drove so much. Well it wasn't long after focusing on that thought that it became a reality and I totaled a car. Fortunately, no one was injured.

Today, I realize how I created that thought, reinforced it through negative self-talk and invited it to happen. I also realized that my thoughts and self-talk are 100 percent under my control.

How can you control things that are under your control?

First you must become aware of what you are saying or thinking. Then you must decide if this is the way you want it to be. If it is, you accept it and move on. If it is not the way you want it to be, reject it. Put a big solid red X through it. Stop it!

You may say something like "I can't." I know, and you know, that with a bit of effort you can have, do or be anything you desire in life. Place, and see, a big solid red X through the words "I cXn't." Stop it as you think of it! That is how you can take control.

Let me share a real-life incident with you where I used the power of the red X to take control of my life.

Online for Life

A few years ago, while at a family Christmas cocktail party, I had a conversation with my wife's cousin. David told me he had just purchased a small airplane on skis. I immediately took advantage of the opportunity and invited him to land on the river by our home to pay us a visit and perhaps take us up for a ride.

Two months later, while finishing my family room, I heard someone knocking on the door. I opened it and there was David. He had flown in with a young man named Troy who was being thanked for a kind deed. Troy, a stranger to both David and his wife, was walking down an Ottawa street and noticed David's wife having a hard time starting her car on Valentine's Day. Being the gentleman that he was, he stopped, helped her start her car, and got her on her way.

David worked as a helicopter mechanic on a military base located outside of Ottawa in Petawawa, and he only made it home on weekends. When he heard about Troy's kindness, he contacted him and offered him a flight in his ski plane over the Gatineau Hills on the following Saturday. Troy had never flown before and was thrilled to be David's passenger.

When David arrived, I sensed he was in a bit of a hurry and that I would not be getting a ride from him that day, as it was just past 4:00 p.m. on a beautiful February day that was coming to an end. When I asked how long he could stay, he told me not long. He had missed Valentine's Day and it was his youngest son's eighteenth birthday. He was taking his wife and son out for dinner and had to be home before 6:00 p.m.

My wife had just left to pick up my sons at the ski hill. I knew she would be home soon, so I delayed David. Finally, they arrived and we all walked down to the river to see David and Troy take off. They checked their fuel and did a walk around, then got in the plane and started it up. They took off with such ease and beauty heading towards Ottawa. Then, they turned around and flew back, as I later learned, to say goodbye, as most pilots do.

There we were, my wife, two sons and I, all excited and waving goodbye to David. Little did we know that we were waving goodbye forever. Within seconds, the plane stalled and crashed less that fifty feet in front of us.

I started running towards the plane and shouting at the kids to run to the house and phone for help. In the meantime, my wife, fearful that the plane would explode, shouted at me to stay away.

As I approached the plane I noticed a small flame coming out of the engine. My only thought at that point was to free David and Troy from the plane in the hope that it might save their lives. I reached into the cockpit to pull David out. I couldn't. I then realized he had his seat belt on. I reached in again to undo it and BANG, the flame blew into a blaze and I felt myself pushed back from the aircraft.

I ran back toward the plane, pushing snow onto the flames with my bare hands. I persisted, knowing all the while there was nothing I could do. Eventually, I just stood there watching the aircraft burn.

It was too late, but within ten minutes neighbors started to arrive on the scene. The fire department, the police, ambulance all followed. The plane was destroyed and so were David and Troy. Nothing could be done. It was too late.

For the next eight hours our house became a control center. We notified David's father. It was not a pleasant task. Police were interrogating my wife, sons, neighbors and people on the other side of the river.

Finally, around 11:00 p.m., the coroner arrived, and using the "Jaws of Life," the bodies were removed from the airplane. What a horrible sight. It wasn't until 2:00 a.m. that everyone finally left and we could go to bed.

Trying to sleep was a torture. I would close my eyes and all I could see was what I had witnessed that day.

I got up, walked around, reflected on the day's events until finally the investigators arrived again. I joined them. Together we investigated the sight in daylight. I insisted the crash site be cleaned up as soon as possible as the plane crashed on the river and it was not my responsibility. Fortunately the Transport people agreed and we made arrangements to have the site cleaned up. That day became another event.

The media obviously took full advantage of this mishap. More and more reporters arrived on the scene, as did many others who wanted to see what happened. Everyone was coming up to me and asking me questions. I just couldn't deal with it. I hid in the house. By the end of the day, everyone was gone and the site was cleaned up. It was over, I thought.

It was Sunday night and I had no energy. I needed some sleep. I went to bed. But again, I could not sleep. I saw what I witnessed on Saturday all over again. I stayed awake all night and then attended a conference the next day.

At the conference, I could not walk without tripping over my own feet. I did not have the energy to pick up my feet and walk. I made it through the day and when I arrived home I went to bed to lie down and rest.

While lying in bed, I started thinking. Then it hit me. I started talking to myself. "Bob, you have dedicated your life to teaching people how to take control of their lives by controlling their thoughts, self-talk, attitudes and reactions. What are you doing to yourself? What happened was not under your control. You did all you could to save them, so why are you letting this incident, that was not under your control, control you like it has over the last three days?"

Realizing what I was saying to myself led me to thinking about my red X theory. I had to put it to use. But, how could I do that while I was suffering through the mental and emotional aftermath of the accident?

As I lay in bed I visualized myself at a high-rise construction site as the heavy equipment was digging the hole for the foundation. The crew was also using a piledriver to hammer in the steel I-beam walls before digging too deep. I saw myself on the top of a steel beam looking up at the hammer head of the piledriver. As I looked at that hammer head I saw a massive, heavy, thick red X waiting to be dropped onto my head. I lifted my arm, tightened up my fist and dropped it onto my forehead with force. I did it again and again, visualizing that red X smashing into my forehead. Within ten drops, I could not lift my arm. I had fallen asleep.

In the morning I woke up, rested. However, I didn't stop there. I continued to control my thoughts using the red X. I am a very emotional person and it took me a few weeks before I could even talk about what happened. I can still remember the incident as if it were yesterday, but I know that there was nothing I could do about it. What happened was not under my control. What *was* under my control were my reactions, my thoughts and my self-talk. I took control over what was under my control and went on with my life.

What about the things that have happened in your life—were they under your control, or not? How did you react? Using the red X, can you see yourself taking control of your life?

Another method you can use is to place an elastic band on your wrist. Every time you have a negative thought or self-talk, pull the band and let it slap you on the wrist. That will send a message to your conscious mind to reject that thought or message.

> *You cannot always control circumstances, but you can control your own thoughts.*
>
> Charles E. Popplestone

Be aware of what you are thinking, saying to yourself or how you react to events that are not under your control. Take the time to eliminate those non-supporting thoughts and sayings, and soon you will be rewarded with the self-control required to live the life of your dreams. All it takes is twenty-one consecutive days of self-discipline to make it a habit.

What about your habits? Are you controlling your habits, or are they controlling you? Negative habits such as self-criticism, procrastination, indecision and fear lead to failure. Negative thoughts prevent us from accomplishing the things we want in life.

Changing your thought process and habits will require a lot of discipline. Discipline is doing what you have to do, even when you don't want to do it. It means respecting the commitment you made to yourself and doing whatever it takes to get it done, when it needs to be done. For example, in Discipline # 2 you made a commitment to yourself to make your decision work. Part of that commitment was to complete all the exercises in this book. Draw up a schedule. Set aside time and do the exercises as scheduled, no matter what. This will be your start to taking control of your life through self-discipline.

So, when it's a beautiful day and your friends want you to go out with them, do what you have to do. Remember that you have a commitment to yourself to work on your goals and your action plan.

Your first step is to decide to take control. This doesn't mean that you don't go out. You might reschedule your plan of action, or, best of all, do your planned work and then reward yourself by going out. This sort of discipline is one of the best habits to have. Not only do you get things done, but you enjoy your rewards more. You have the satisfaction of having respected your commitment to yourself. A habit that gets rewarded gets repeated.

What are the ineffective or bad habits that you want to get rid of? What are the things you want to change in your life? Write them down. You can come back and add on others as you think of them.

Ineffective or bad habits that I want to overcome:

_____

_____

_____

_____

_____

Now, identify the new behavior, the effective habits and improvements that you want in your life. What would be good replacement habits? For example, I used to smoke and realized that it was not good for my health. So I sat back and thought what would be good for my health as a replacement habit. I found that jogging each morning helped me quit smoking. I also had previously replaced procrastination with a "do it now" attitude. Write out the desired behaviors and habits that you will work on. You can come back and add to your list later, too.

Effective habits that I want to master:

_____

_____

_____

_____

_____

Replacing the ineffective habits with effective ones can be a challenging process. Nathaniel Emmons said, "Habit is either the best of servants or the worst of masters." Later in this book I will guide you through a simple 30-day process to successfully change your habits and make them your servants.

Many of my behaviors and habits developed over time. I really learned to master discipline by following the prescribed method of reading *The Greatest Salesman in the World* by Og Mandino. I applied the 30-day discipline that eventually made me a slave to some good habits and attitudes.

The prescribed method was to read one of ten short scrolls, three times a day for thirty days before proceeding onto the next scroll. If you missed a morning, noon or evening reading, you had to start that scroll over again from day one. It seemed pretty easy, at first.

A book that could have been read in an afternoon took me eighteen months to complete, as prescribed. But the results astonished me. What do you think would happen to you if you kept repeating the same positive message to yourself three times a day for thirty days?

One of the disciplines that helped me take control of my life was the habit of highlighting what I read for future reference, and writing down my thoughts. I started a journal. I recommend that you write your thoughts at the end of each discipline in this book and highlight your favorite points as you go. You may want to look back to what your thoughts were at various times, or refer to certain points. As Confucius said, "The palest ink lasts longer than the strongest memory."

Working through this book, you have defined your vision of success, you have decided to act, and you have identified new habits to develop. What steps will you now take in order to take control of your life?

I will take control of my life by taking the following steps:

I will read and do the exercises in this book, to the best of my ability, for _____ (minutes or hours) _____ (per day or week) starting today.

Signature: _____

Date: _____

Summary ∽

Discipline #3: Take Control of Your Life

You are capable of controlling your thoughts and states of mind.

Your thoughts control your attitude and how you react to situations. Your thoughts are you!

If you fail to control your mind, how can you control anything else?

To take control of our lives we must first identify the things we have no control over and the things that we can control.

Your first step is to *decide* to take control.

Your beliefs drive your attitude. Your attitude drives everything!

Become aware of what you are saying and what you are thinking, as your thoughts of today are your realities of tomorrow.

If it is not the way you want it to be, reject it. Put a big solid red X through it. Stop it! Replace it with the way you want it to be.

Discipline yourself—do what you have to do even when you don't want to do it, and then reward yourself.

Identify the habits that are working for you (effective) and those that are working against you (ineffective).

Habits are not easy to break, and it takes up to 30 days to master a new habit. So start now!

You will need commitment, discipline and determination to change your habits, but the rewards are worth it.

Write down everything. Create a journal to refer to.

When you read, highlight key points for future reference.

Decide what steps you will take to take control of your life.

Personalize and sign your time and frequency commitment (discipline) to completing all the exercises in this book.

Thought space

_____
_____
_____
_____
_____
_____
_____
_____
_____
_____
_____
_____
_____
_____
_____
_____
_____
_____
_____
_____
_____
_____

Discipline # 4
Know Yourself

*No person has a chance to enjoy permanent
success until he begins to look in a mirror
for the real cause of all his mistakes.*

Napoleon Hill

We all bear the influence of our friends, schools, parents—and our total environment. Some of this baggage is positive while some of it is negative. We accept a lot of it as the absolute truth and the way life must be. This has caused us to set our own limitations, most of them externally influenced. But are these things that we have learned really true?

If you take the time to know yourself, you become internally driven. Know yourself, from the inside out—your values, your motivators and de-motivators, your strengths and your weaknesses. Realize how you see yourself.

As adults we can decide who and what we will and will not be. Take advantage of this power. Your greatest strength and direction will come from inside you, not from the outside world.

We are easily influenced by people and circumstances, and forget sometimes who we really are and what is important to us. These forces can control us and force us into a mold of conformity, diminishing any thought or action that might develop our individuality and creativity.

If we repeatedly hear the words "you can't," it's easy to be convinced that we cannot achieve our dreams. If we hear "anyone who makes a lot of money is a crook," we may be influenced not to make any significant amount of money. On the other hand, a positive message like "anyone who controls their spending can accumulate money" would encourage us to control our spending.

You have the right to select what motivates you and to understand your feelings. The choices you make will direct the course you follow in life.

Over the years I have had the opportunity to complete a variety of profiling tests. These tests can tell participants about their strengths and weaknesses, their personality type and the sorts of work that may suit them. I have learned so much about myself this way that I recommend you take advantage of these opportunities to learn about yourself.

As I mentioned in Discipline #1 (Know Your Rights), no one is perfect. We all have our strengths and weaknesses—that's human nature. What we need to know is who we are and what our strengths and weaknesses are. This will guide us into doing things we enjoy and avoiding things we don't. We will be able to set and achieve realistic goals. We will live a happy life, a life of our choice.

If you are like Andrij the student, and you have no concept of who or what you are, your journey into the future will be uncertain and dependent upon circumstances—circumstances that are not all under your control. You will wander aimlessly through life. Without a well-defined identity, your ability to succeed will depend on luck. But success is not about luck. Defining your identity will keep you focused as you set priorities, organize tasks, deal with emergencies and accomplish challenges in your personal and business life.

The first step in defining your identity involves self-awareness—

seeing yourself as you really are. It involves being honest with yourself. Taking inventory of yourself can be an uncomfortable and even painful experience, but you must do it in order to move on.

On the following pages you will find some exercises. I would like you to look inside, or into that mirror in front of you, and complete these exercises before proceeding any further. Sit in a comfortable place, and write down as much as you can. Sleep on it, and then go back and add to your answers. Make any additions or changes that you wish—this is your inventory.

There are no wrong answers, but be honest with yourself. The answers are for you only. They will help you better understand yourself—to know who you really are. This is the foundation to the house of success that you are building.

Who Am I?

Over the years and in many speaking engagements, I have recommended the following exercise to help participants discover their real "identity." David Sandler goes into great detail with this exercise and the subject of identity in his book *You Can't Teach a Kid to Ride a Bike at a Seminar* (see Bibliography).

We all play a variety of roles in life. What are some of the roles that you play or positions you hold in life, i.e., parent, spouse, student, manager…?

Identify and rate your roles from 1 to 10 on how you see or feel about yourself in each role, 1 being "poor" and 10 being "great."

What You "R" (Roles)	Rating
_____	_____
_____	_____
_____	_____
_____	_____

_____   _____
_____   _____
_____   _____
_____   _____
_____   _____
_____   _____

Average Rating of What You "R"   _____

When answering the next question, imagine yourself alone, with no roles. Who is this person? Look into the mirror; what do you see? Are you honest, sincere, positive, committed, loving, caring, giving or respectful? Are you jealous, negative, dishonest, humble, uncommitted, disrespectful or living in fear? Try to list as many points about yourself as you can. You can always come back to this page and add to it. Do your best for now, but do it.

Rate yourself from 1 to 10 on how you see or feel about yourself without your roles; again, 1 being "poor" and 10 being "great."

Who You "I" (Identity)	Rating
_____	_____
_____	_____
_____	_____
_____	_____
_____	_____
_____	_____
_____	_____
_____	_____
_____	_____

Average Rating of Who You "I"   _____

Where is your highest rating?

What You "R" _____ or Who You "I" _____

If the highest rating is your role "R," beware. What you "R" has become your identity. What would happen if you lost your role(s) or position(s) tomorrow? What would your identity be then?

If your "I" rating is higher than your role "R" rating, congratulations! You are on the right track. You are approaching life from the inside out, and that is what matters most.

Your identity and how you feel about yourself is most important.

David Sandler explained it most effectively by saying, "You can perform in your roles (R) only in a manner that is consistent with how we see yourself conceptually (I). In other words, your role corresponds to your identity rating, every time."

This means if you see yourself as a "3" you will perform in your roles as a "3." But, if you see yourself as a "10" you will perform as a "10." It all starts from the inside and how you see or feel about yourself. That is where your self-esteem and self-confidence come from.

Self-esteem and self-confidence will give you the courage and discipline to do the things you always wanted to do. Lack of self-confidence or self-esteem will cause you to procrastinate, not make decisions, take little or no risk, and leave life to chance.

Who is the most important person in the world?

_____

What would I like to rate that person as?
A ____ (1—10) by _____ (date)

Focus on your "I"—your internal identity. That is where you will experience the greatest of miracles.

Online for Life

Thank you for being honest with yourself, and disciplined in completing the previous exercises. The following exercises will help you to discover yourself while developing plans to improve your "I" rating, your self-confidence and self-esteem.

Continue to complete the following exercises in the order that they appear and you will get to know yourself even better. You will also become increasingly self-disciplined.

What Are My Values?

Your fundamental beliefs are your values. Values are also known as principles, ideals, convictions or purposes. Your beliefs are important to you, and will motivate you. The following exercise will help you set your life's priorities.

Values are the basis for the laws that govern society. Murder, theft and assault, for example, violate society's common values. Society's values, and by extension its laws, provide us with the structure that helps us organize our lives.

By clarifying your values, you create a structure upon which you can build your personal and business life. You must understand your values before you can master the rest of the disciplines in this book.

The following table lists many of the things that motivate people. Rate each according to how much you value it: always, often, sometimes, seldom or never. Then go back and rank your "Always Valued" checks in order of their importance to you. It is these values that will help you find your passion and motivate you to the realization of your dreams.

The 12 Disciplines for Living Your Dreams

Rank	Motivator	Always Valued	Often Valued	Sometimes Valued	Seldom Valued	Never Valued
_____	Advancement					
_____	Adventure					
_____	Aesthetics					
_____	Authority/power					
_____	Challenge					
_____	Change/variety					
_____	Community					
_____	Competence					
_____	Competition					
_____	Creativity					
_____	Decision making					
_____	Excitement					
_____	Family					
_____	Freedom					
_____	Friendships					
_____	Group affiliations					
_____	Helping others					
_____	Helping society					
_____	Independence					
_____	Influencing people					
_____	Intelligence					
_____	Job security					

Rank	Motivator	Always Valued	Often Valued	Sometimes Valued	Seldom Valued	Never Valued
_____	Knowledge					
_____	Location of home					
_____	Location of work					
_____	Money					
_____	Moral standards					
_____	New ideas/things					
_____	Personal contact					
_____	Personal security					
_____	Physical challenge					
_____	Public contact					
_____	Recognition					
_____	Religious beliefs					
_____	Salary level					
_____	Stability					
_____	Status					
_____	Supervision					
_____	Tranquility					
_____	Working alone					
_____	Working under pressure					
_____	Working with people					
_____	Others:					

You can now answer the following three questions:

What is important to me now, in the short term?

_____

_____

_____

_____

What is important to me later, in the medium term?

_____

_____

_____

_____

What is important to me in my life, over the long term?

_____

_____

_____

_____

Personal Evaluation

This exercise is meant to help you see your situation, understand why you rate yourself as you do, and decide what actions you can take to improve your ratings. It will give you a base to measure your progress as you rate yourself in the future.

Rate yourself from 1 to 10 on how you see or feel about yourself; again, 1 is "poor" and 10 is "great."

Physical: _____

For example: appearance, medical check-ups, exercise programs, weight control, nutrition

Why did you rate yourself like this?

_____

_____

_____

_____

Identify the positive factors.

_____

_____

_____

_____

Identify areas for improvement.

_____

_____

_____

_____

What actions must I take to be closer to a 10?

_____

_____

_____

_____

_____

_____

Family: _____

For example: listening habits, forgiving attitude, good role model, time together, supportive of others, respectful, loving

Why did you rate yourself like this?

_____

_____

_____

_____

Identify the positive factors.

_____

_____

_____

_____

Identify areas for improvement.

_____

_____

_____

_____

What actions must I take to be closer to a 10?

_____

_____

_____

_____

_____

_____

Financial: _____

For example: earnings, savings and investments, budget, adequate insurance, charge accounts

Why did you rate yourself like this?

_____

_____

_____

_____

Identify the positive factors.

_____

_____

_____

_____

Identify areas for improvement.

_____

_____

_____

_____

What actions must I take to be closer to a 10?

_____

_____

_____

_____

_____

_____

Social: _____

For example: sense of humor, listening habits, self-confidence, manners, caring

Why did you rate yourself like this?

_____

_____

_____

_____

Identify the positive factors.

_____

_____

_____

_____

Identify areas for improvement.

_____

_____

_____

_____

What actions must I take to be closer to a 10?

_____

_____

_____

_____

_____

_____

Spiritual: _____

For example: inner peace, sense of purpose, prayer, religious study, belief in God

Why did you rate yourself like this?

_____

_____

_____

_____

Identify the positive factors.

_____

_____

_____

_____

Identify areas for improvement.

_____

_____

_____

_____

What actions must I take to be closer to a 10?

_____

_____

_____

_____

_____

_____

Mental: _____

For example: imagination, attitude, continuing education, reading, curiosity

Why did you rate yourself like this?

_____

_____

_____

_____

Identify the positive factors.

_____

_____

_____

_____

Identify areas for improvement.

_____

_____

_____

_____

What actions must I take to be closer to a 10?

_____

_____

_____

_____

_____

_____

Career*:* _____

For example: job satisfaction, effectiveness, job training, understanding job purpose, competence

Why did you rate yourself like this?

_____
_____
_____
_____

Identify the positive factors.

_____
_____
_____
_____

Identify areas for improvement.

_____
_____
_____
_____

What actions must I take to be closer to a 10?

_____
_____
_____
_____
_____
_____

Now that you have had a good look at yourself, take a break before completing the following list of your assets and liabilities.

List of Assets and Liabilities

Strengths	**Weaknesses**
I am good at:	*I need improvement in:*
1. _____	1. _____
2. _____	2. _____
3. _____	3. _____
4. _____	4. _____
5. _____	5. _____
6. _____	6. _____
7. _____	7. _____
8. _____	8. _____
9. _____	9. _____
10. _____	10. _____

Here is an important question: Did you start listing weaknesses or strengths? If you started listing weaknesses, what does that tell you about your self-confidence and self-esteem?

Asset Message: Refer to and reread, relish and dwell on these strengths (assets) constantly. They will take you anywhere you want to go, providing you with the energy you need to keep moving forward. Your strengths represent your self-worth.

Liability Message: Pick the top three weaknesses and do something about them. Forget the rest. No one is perfect, nor is that goal realistic.

Online for Life

Understanding My Motivation

Think about an experience in your life that you really enjoyed. Then think about an episode when you had to do something you didn't enjoy. What do those experiences tell you about yourself?

What motivates me?

_____
_____
_____

What *de*motivates me?

_____
_____
_____

What are some conditioning influences that affect me?

_____
_____
_____

What are some negative messages that motivate me? (i.e., "You can't do it!")

_____
_____
_____

What are some positive messages that motivate me? (i.e., "You *can* do it!")

_____
_____
_____

The 12 Disciplines for Living Your Dreams

Do you know yourself a little better now? I hope so. Naturally, there is more to know. For example, why do we sometimes not move forward toward our dreams? Why do we procrastinate? The problem is that we all set our own limitations, mostly because of one thing: fear—fear of the unknown, fear of rejection, fear of failure, fear of what others will say... and the list goes on.

Because of fear, many of us don't take action toward our dreams. We procrastinate. Fear paralyzes the faculty of reason, destroys the faculty of imagination, kills self-reliance, undermines enthusiasm, discourages initiative, leads to uncertainty of purpose, encourages procrastination, and makes self-control difficult. Fear removes the charm from a personality, destroys ambition, clouds memory and invites failure. It leads to sleeplessness, misery and unhappiness.

Fear is nothing more than a state of mind, and everyone has the ability to control his or her own state of mind. Do you think your fears are the same as everyone else's? Are your fears my fears? Your fears are your fears and no one else's! Your fears exist only in your mind. Only you can overcome those fears.

The three biggest obstacles in life are indecision, doubt and fear. Indecision is the seedling of fear. Indecision crystallizes into doubt, and together the two become fear. We fear so many things, from failure to death. Some fears are justified. But other unnecessary fears can take root and grow unless you get rid of the indecision and doubt that sow the seeds of fear. But before you can master fear, you must know its name, habits and where it comes from.

For example, when I was in my early twenties I was afraid to try public speaking. I was concerned that my language and my appearance were not good enough to stand in front of a crowd and speak. I dreaded rejection and criticism as a result of being criticized as a teenager by my friends. This fear prevented me from doing something I really wanted to do—to earn more by selling through speaking to large groups.

Then, with some coaching, I developed enough self-confidence to finally give it a try. And the audience applauded! My fear could have set me back forever. Instead, I got on stage again the next day and spoke in front of another group of people. I faced my biggest fear head-on and I got my first standing ovation! That was enough to give me the confidence to keep going, and to accomplish my dream of becoming a professional speaker.

The following exercises are intended to help you master your fears. What are your five biggest fears?

Fear #1

_____

_____

_____

What has this fear prevented me from doing?

_____

_____

_____

What experiences caused this fear?

_____

_____

_____

If I face this fear head-on, what is the worst thing that can happen?

_____

_____

_____

What can I do to overcome this fear?

_____

_____

_____

Fear #2

What has this fear prevented me from doing?

_____

_____

_____

What experiences caused this fear?

_____

_____

_____

If I face this fear head-on, what is the worst thing that can happen?

_____

_____

_____

What can I do to overcome this fear?

_____

_____

_____

Fear #3

What has this fear prevented me from doing?

_____

_____

_____

What experiences caused this fear?

_____

_____

_____

If I face this fear head-on, what is the worst thing that can happen?

_____

_____

_____

What can I do to overcome this fear?

_____

_____

_____

Fear #4

What has this fear prevented me from doing?

_____

_____

_____

What experiences caused this fear?

_____

_____

_____

If I face this fear head-on, what is the worst thing that can happen?

_____

_____

_____

What can I do to overcome this fear?

_____

_____

_____

Fear #5

What has this fear prevented me from doing?

_____

_____

_____

What experiences caused this fear?

_____

_____

_____

If I face this fear head-on, what is the worst thing that can happen?

_____

_____

_____

What can I do to overcome this fear?

_____

_____

_____

Here are some quotations on the topic of fear. When I need courage to face fear, I review these. You may want to refer to these quotes when you are held back because of fear.

Do the thing you fear most and you will control fear.

Bobby Charleton

Do the thing you fear to do and keep doing it; that is the quickest and surest way ever discovered to conquer fear.

Dale Carnegie

We have nothing to fear but fear itself.

Franklin D. Roosevelt

Courage is not the absence of fear, but rather the judgment that something is more important than fear.

Ambrose Redbone

It is the mind that maketh good of ill, that maketh wretch or happy, rich or poor.

Edmund Spenser

Worry is a state of mind based upon fear. It paralyzes one's reasoning faculty, destroys self-confidence and initiative.

Napoleon Hill

Failure will never overtake you if your determination to succeed is strong enough.

Og Mandino

I would rather be a failure in something that I love than a success in something that I didn't.

George Burns

Our greatest glory is not in never failing, but in rising every time we fall.

Confucius

Develop success from failures. Discouragement and failure are two of the secret stepping stones to success.

Dale Carnegie

One of the things we fear most is failure. You must realize, though, that you learn from failure. You can overcome the fear of failure by giving yourself permission to fail. Keep in mind that success is based on good judgment and good judgment is based on experience. And how does one get experience? Right—through failure.

You will need courage, because the only way to eliminate fear is to face it, head-on. Have courage and develop self-confidence through the elimination of fear. You can do it!

The first and best victory is to conquer self. To be conquered by self is, of all things, the most shameful and vile.

Plato

Congratulations. You have completed some difficult exercises. You have demonstrated your commitment to your decision to lead the life of your choice. You have also demonstrated your commitment to take control of your life and to know yourself. You have graduated from the first four disciplines. Keep up the good work. You will find the rest of this book, and the exercises it contains, easier. Now move on to Discipline # 5 (Know What You Want Out of Life) *after* you take a break, reward yourself and celebrate your accomplishments.

The following is a message for those who did not complete the exercises on the previous pages.

A lot of people don't succeed in life and know all the reasons why they don't. They have airtight alibis to explain their lack of achievement. As you read the following list of alibis, consider how many, if any, you use. Remember that the philosophy of this book considers every one of these alibis to be obsolete.

IF I didn't have a spouse and a family...

IF I had enough pull...

IF I had money...

IF I had a good education...

IF I could get a job...

IF I had good health...

IF I only had time...

IF times were better...

IF other people understood me...

IF conditions around me were only different...

IF I could live my life over again...

IF I did not fear what "they" would say...

IF I had been given a chance...

IF I had a chance...

IF other people didn't have it in for me...

IF nothing happens to stop me...

IF I were only younger...

IF I could only do what I want...

IF I had been born rich...

IF I could meet the right people...

IF I had the talent some people have...

IF I dared assert myself...

IF I only had embraced past opportunities...

The 12 Disciplines for Living Your Dreams

IF people didn't get on my nerves...

IF I didn't have to keep the house and look after the children...

IF I could save some money...

IF the boss only appreciated me...

IF I only had someone to help me...

IF my family understood me...

IF I lived in a big city...

IF I could just get started...

IF I only were free...

IF I had the personality of some people...

IF I were not so fat...

IF my talents were known...

IF I could just get a break...

IF I could only get out of debt...

IF I hadn't failed...

IF I only knew how...

IF everyone didn't oppose me...

IF I didn't have so many worries...

IF I could marry the right person...

IF people weren't so dumb...

IF my family were not so extravagant...

IF I were sure of myself...

IF luck were not against me...

IF I had not been born under the wrong star...

IF it were not true that "what is to be will be"...

IF I did not have to work so hard...

IF I hadn't lost my money...

IF I lived in a different neighborhood...

IF I didn't have a "past"...

IF I only had a business of my own...

IF other people would only listen to me...

But consider this…

IF I had the courage to see myself as I really am, I would find out what is wrong with the way I am approaching life, and correct it. Then I might have a chance to profit from my mistakes and learn something from others.

A lot people are lazy and not adequately committed to improving their lives. They may have made a decision (Discipline #2) but they didn't respect their personal commitment. Therefore, they just glanced over the previous exercises and decided to do them later. The problem is that later never comes. Their lives will remain the same simply because they didn't take these first steps towards taking control of their lives: writing things down (Discipline #3) and getting to know themselves better (Discipline #4).

It is not too late to complete the exercises. Discipline yourself immediately. Simply sit down somewhere comfortable and start, now. Take that first step towards improving the quality of your life. Complete all the previous exercises before moving on.

Just remember one thing—it is your life and your choice.

Summary ⌒

Discipline # 4: Know Yourself

If you have no concept of who you are, your journey into the future will be uncertain.

Defining your identity will keep you focused as you later set priorities, organize tasks, deal with emergencies and accomplish challenges in your personal and business life. Your identity and how you feel about yourself is most important. Who am I, without roles?

Look inside, what do you see? What are my values, how do I see and feel about myself, what are my strengths and weaknesses, what motivates me, what demotivates me, what are my fears and how will I overcome them?

Fear is nothing more than a state of mind, and every human being has the ability to completely control his or her own states of mind.

Indecision is the seedling of fear. Indecision crystallizes into doubt, and together the two become fear.

Success is based on good judgment. Good judgment is based on experience. And how do you get experience? Through failure.

Lazy people have all the reasons and airtight alibis to explain their lack of achievement.

IF I had the courage to see myself as I really am, I would find out what is wrong with the way I am approaching life, and correct it.

Thought space

_____

_____

_____

_____

_____
_____
_____
_____
_____
_____
_____
_____
_____
_____
_____
_____
_____
_____
_____
_____

Discipline # 5
Know What You Want Out of Life

If you don't have a dream and I don't have a dream, how are we going to make a dream come true?

Mary Martin

In Discipline #1 we discussed our rights. Our first right is to our dreams, desires and expectations.

In this chapter you will take the time to think about your dreams, desires and expectations, and to write them down. You must know what you want out of life in order to get it. Without knowing what you want you would go through life aimlessly, like a ship without a rudder. Until your dreams are written down on paper, they will merely be wishes.

When I was twenty-two years old I took a sick day from work, as I was truly sick at how my life was getting nowhere. I sat down at the dining room table and asked myself a very important question: What do I want out of life?

As I sat there thinking, I picked up a pencil and started writing down my thoughts on a pad of paper. I wrote down every thought that came to mind, no matter how ridiculous, or impossible, it might have been. I just kept writing and writing. Before long, I had filled the whole pad of paper with all of my thoughts, dreams and life desires. I no longer felt ill. I felt great. I felt a sense of direction.

You too can experience that same sensation by completing the following exercises. These exercises will become the basis for the rest of your life. Strive to come up with the most complete and descriptive lists possible.

Start with your List of Dreams. Find a comfortable place where you will not be disturbed. You may want to play some inspirational or relaxing music to help you along. Have some extra paper and pencils with you.

List your dreams—write down every possible and crazy dream that comes to mind. In order for this exercise to be effective you must accept that nothing is impossible. There are no barriers, obstacles or excuses why something can't happen. The objective is to write down every thought or desire that comes to your mind, no matter how silly, impossible or crazy it is. This is not a test; there are no wrong answers.

Write down everything you'd love to have, do or be. What type of career do you want, with what sort of employer and team workers? Where do you want to travel? Do you want to fly or sail around the world, or live in a castle on the Rhine River? Do you want to be physically and mentally fit, be a superstar, a salesperson? Would you like to earn a quarter-million dollars a year?

You may want to be married, live on a farm, have a large family, stay home and raise the family, be a volunteer worker, a recognized person in your community, a teacher, a musician, a poet... Write down whatever your heart desires. Just keep writing. Everything is possible.

Spend at least an hour writing down your life dreams. Take the time and make the best of it. Have fun!

Your objective is to write all of your dreams and desires for the next six months; for the next year; five years; and for life. Write, write, write and keep writing. Identify everything you want to have, be or do at some point in your life. Remember, there are no wrong answers and this list is for your reference only. It doesn't have to be neat or organized in any way. Just write every thought that comes to mind. Sleep on it and add more the next day if you like. Keep in mind that there are no barriers and that nothing is impossible. Go ahead and start!

These suggestions might help you write your list of dreams:

Examples of Dreams

Travel and Vacations	Children and Family
(where and how)	*(education, activities, shared time)*
Automobile	Friendship
(kind, color, options)	*(respect, helping others)*
House	Health
(size, style, extras)	*(body weight, exercise)*
Money	Mind
(savings, net worth, investments)	*(self-esteem, knowledge)*
Career	Environment
(salary increase, promotions,	Sports
new job, own business)	Relationships
Physical	
(personal development)	

My dreams, desires and expectations of life:

_____

_____

_____

_____

_____

_____

_____

_____

My dreams, desires and expectations of life (continued):

_____

_____

_____

_____

_____

_____

The 12 Disciplines for Living Your Dreams

My dreams, desires and expectations of life (continued):

_____

_____

_____

_____

_____

_____

_____

_____

_____

_____

_____

_____

_____

_____

_____

_____

_____

_____

_____

_____

_____

_____

_____

_____

_____

_____

_____

_____

_____

_____

My dreams, desires and expectations of life (continued):

_____

_____

_____

_____

_____

_____

_____

_____

What great thing would you attempt if you knew that you couldn't fail?

_____

_____

_____

_____

_____

_____

_____

_____

_____

_____

_____

_____

Please do not go past this point unless you have written out *all* of your dreams, desires and expectations of life. Think of this as your last chance. Go back and add any last dreams, desires and expectations.

Now do the same exercise for your retirement years. Retirement means something different to each of us. Your desires for your retirement are your choice. So, take some time here and write out your retirement expectations, desires and dreams. Write as descriptively as possible and include everything that comes to mind. Don't limit yourself, just write everything you can imagine having, being or doing in your retirement. Then sleep on it and add to the list in the morning.

My retirement expectations:

_____

_____

_____

_____

_____

_____

_____

_____

_____

_____

_____

_____

_____

Now that you have a good idea of how you want to spend your retirement years, complete the following lifeline. Draw a vertical line under "retirement age" and write the age at which you will retire.

We all know that we won't live forever. As much as we don't like to think about it, I would like you to write the age at which you think you will die on the extreme right of the line, under the word "die."

Your Lifeline

	Born	Indicate Present Age	Retirement Age	Die?

Age 0

You notice that the lifeline starts at age 0, when you were born, and now you have an indication of when it will end. Next, draw a vertical line through the lifeline scale at your present age and write that age below it.

Then scribble out the past, everything between age 0 and your present age. There is nothing you can do about this period. It is gone. The only thing those years represent is your experience.

How much time do you have left to accomplish what you want out of life?

_____

How much time do you have prior to retirement?

_____

Today is the first day of the rest of your life!

I encourage you to make the best of the time remaining. Part II of this book will help you decide how to best use that time. For now, be aware of your lifeline, where you are in it, and how much time you have left to make things happen.

Now, imagine that you have just been infected with a deadly virus and you have only six months to live. Too many people wait for retirement or notice of illness to actually do the things they always wanted to do, but never did. If you only had six months left to live, how would you want to spend your remaining time?

The 12 Disciplines for Living Your Dreams

How would you like to spend your remaining time?

_____

_____

_____

_____

_____

_____

_____

Time is all we have. We do not know when that time will expire, but we must make the best use of it while we can. Take the time each morning to be thankful that you were given another morning to face the challenges of a new day. For you never know what tomorrow may bring.

Our cousin David did not know it was his time when his plane stalled and crashed. I am sure he would have preferred an extension on life, even if it were just to take his wife and son out for dinner that night and tell them how much he loved them. Unfortunately, David's time expired without warning or reason.

When someone leaves us suddenly, we think about all the things we should have shared with that person, in actions or words, while they were alive, but didn't. Don't wait until it is too late to let people know how you feel about them. You may not get another chance. But, while you have a chance, look inside and answer a couple of difficult questions for yourself.

How would you like to be remembered after you're gone?

_____

_____

_____

_____

_____

How do you think you would be remembered if you died tomorrow?

_____

_____

_____

_____

_____

Here is your chance to define how you want to be remembered after you pass away. What would you like your family, friends and work associates to say in your eulogy?

Family:

_____

_____

_____

_____

_____

Friends:

_____

_____

_____

_____

_____

Work associates:

_____

_____

_____

_____

_____

What behavior changes do you need to make to have the previous words spoken honestly?

_____

_____

_____

_____

_____

If a statue was built in your honor, what accomplishments would you want to have listed on the plaque?

_____

_____

_____

_____

_____

Congratulations, you have completed the first steps towards self-motivation and personal leadership. Take the time to recognize your accomplishments. Treat yourself to a special occasion. You deserve to be rewarded for the effort and discipline extended.

And remember…

Whatever the mind can conceive and believe, it can achieve.

Napoleon Hill

Summary

Discipline # 5: Know What You Want Out of Life

List all your dreams, desires and expectations as if nothing were impossible.

What great thing would you attempt if you knew that you couldn't fail?

How much time do you have left to accomplish what you want out of life?

What are your retirement expectations?

How much time do you have prior to retirement?

If you were told you had six months to live, how would you live them?

How would you want your family, friends and work associates to remember you? What would you want them to say in your eulogy?

What behavior changes do you need to make to become the person in that eulogy?

Thought space

_____

_____

_____

_____

_____

_____

_____

_____

_____

_____

_____

Part II

⌒

Creating Your Future,
One Step at a Time

"Most people spend
more time planning
their vacation than
the rest of their lives."

Mary Kay Ash

Continuing ⌒

If we all did the things that we are capable of doing, we would literally astound ourselves.

Thomas A. Edison

In Part I we explored the definition of success, attitude and motivation, and followed the first five disciplines to self-motivation and personal leadership. If you are serious about doing something about your life, you have completed all the exercises to the best of your ability. You now possess an outline of what motivates you, what your values are, and what your strengths and weaknesses and fears are. You have an extensive list of your life dreams, and you have thought ahead about what sort of person you want to be remembered as.

You accomplished a lot by completing these exercises. You demonstrated that you can make a decision, and that you have the courage to take control of your life. You demonstrated that you have vision by outlining your desires and expectations. You completed the exercises, so you are persistent and disciplined. You demonstrated your honesty by being honest with yourself. You have completed the first steps towards self-motivation and personal leadership.

Take a moment to reflect upon your accomplishments in Part I. They are significant.

If you did not complete the exercises in Part I, think how satisfied you would feel if you had completed them. It's not too late to go back and do the exercises now. Part II of this book will mean nothing to you unless you complete Part I.

In Part II: Creating Your Future, One Step at a Time, you will take what you have done in Part I and mold it into an action plan. You will identify, group and prioritize your most significant dreams and turn them into goals. You will create a goal logbook and create an action plan to accomplish each goal. You will learn to daily reinforce and monitor your actions and goals.

This part of the process will also require a lot of work, determination and persistence. Leaders don't give up. Continue the discipline of writing, completing each exercise as you meet it. Before long you'll be where you want to be, have what you want to have, and be doing what you want to do. Remember two things: there are no wrong answers and nothing is impossible.

Discipline # 6
Group, Categorize and Prioritize ⌒

*If you don't know where you are going,
you will probably end up somewhere
else.*

Mark Twain

Now it is time to "go online," to take what you have done and put your work into a structure that will enable you to live your dreams.

When I was twenty-two and spent a "sick" day at home writing out my dreams, I started to feel great. Once they were all down on paper, I took a lunch break and then wondered how I could possibly organize those dreams. I sat there and thought. It then came to me. If I could position all "like" dreams together, I could identify this grouping with a name that would provide a form or organization. Hence, grouping and categorizing.

Once I had all my dreams grouped and categorized by name, things were easier to see. As I looked at my accomplishments, I saw something that really woke me up. It was the realization that I really could "make it happen," as the first steps of my life plan were now staring me in the face.

Quickly, I realized that most of my category dreams were linked to each other. I realized that by numbering each dream in order of priority, the action would then lead to the accomplishment of another dream in the same or different category. As I started to number them, a plan became evident. Hence, prioritizing.

In Discipline #5 (Know What You Want Out of Life) you listed a lot of dreams, desires and expectations. Now, I would like you to go back to your dreams and group them by activity type and categorize each group by giving it a title. For example, you might decide that your dreams cluster under the headings of travel, family, career and finances.

On the following pages are charts on which you can categorize your dreams. Look at your dream list in Discipline #5 and decide on your category titles. Write those titles on the following charts. Then go back to your main list and select the dreams that fall into each category. You can do this with a different color highlighter pen for each category. Then write those dreams on the category chart.

You can be brief here because you will expand on your dreams when you create a goal logbook (Discipline #8).

Category	Dream List	Date/Age
— _____	— _____	_____
	— _____	_____
	— _____	_____
	— _____	_____
	— _____	_____
	— _____	_____
	— _____	_____
	— _____	_____
	— _____	_____
	— _____	_____
	— _____	_____

The 12 Disciplines for Living Your Dreams

Category	Dream List	Date/Age
—_____	—_____	_____
	—_____	_____
	—_____	_____
	—_____	_____
	—_____	_____
	—_____	_____
	—_____	_____
	—_____	_____

Category	Dream List	Date/Age
—_____	—_____	_____
	—_____	_____
	—_____	_____
	—_____	_____
	—_____	_____
	—_____	_____
	—_____	_____

Category	Dream List	Date/Age
—_____	—_____	_____
	—_____	_____
	—_____	_____
	—_____	_____
	—_____	_____
	—_____	_____

Online for Life

Category	Dream List	Date/Age
— _____	— _____	_____
	— _____	_____
	— _____	_____
	— _____	_____
	— _____	_____
	— _____	_____
	— _____	_____
	— _____	_____

Category	Dream List	Date/Age
— _____	— _____	_____
	— _____	_____
	— _____	_____
	— _____	_____
	— _____	_____
	— _____	_____
	— _____	_____
	— _____	_____

Category	Dream List	Date/Age
— _____	— _____	_____
	— _____	_____
	— _____	_____
	— _____	_____
	— _____	_____
	— _____	_____
	— _____	_____
	— _____	_____

Now that you have your categories organized, the next step is to prioritize their contents.

When I was at this stage and looking at my different categories, I noticed that some of my dreams listed under career, family and travel categories were interrelated. I realized that if I secured the type of job I desired with national responsibility, I would realize two other dreams – home ownership and seeing Canada, my top family and travel dreams at the time. Take the time and review what you wrote. You too will see the beginnings of a plan.

Start with your first category. Which dream do you most want to accomplish? Call that number 1. Continue down the list until all the dreams in that category are numbered in order of importance. Now view the dreams from a planning, or implementation, point of view. Should the numbering change because of implementation logic? If so, change them. Carry on and sort the contents of all your categories in this way.

Now it is time to prioritize the categories. Which category is the most important to you, today? Call that number 1. Which ones would be nice to have, but are not as important? Assign those a lower priority.

Now view the categories from a planning, or implementation, point of view. Should the numbering change because of implementation logic? If so, change them.

Now place your dreams on a timeline. Go back and review the list you just made. To the right of each dream, based on its priority, write the date (or your age) by which you would like to have this dream realized.

Once you have done this, use the space starting on page 116 to describe in detail your top three dreams for each time period. These will be the dreams you will work on in the next discipline, and until you make them a reality.

Online for Life

Describe your top three dreams, in detail, for the following periods:

For the next three to six months...

1. _____
_____
_____
_____

2. _____
_____
_____
_____

3. _____
_____
_____
_____

For the next twelve months...

1. _____
_____
_____
_____

2. _____
_____
_____
_____

3. _____

_____

_____

_____

For the next three to five years...

1. _____

_____

_____

_____

2. _____

_____

_____

_____

3. _____

_____

_____

_____

For my retirement years...

1. _____

_____

_____

_____

2. _____

_____

_____

_____

3. _____

_____

_____

_____

For life...

1. _____

_____

_____

_____

2. _____

_____

_____

_____

3. _____

_____

_____

_____

Please do not go past this point until you have filled out *all* of the time periods. Think of this as your last chance. Go back and review your dreams and retirement expectations. All the answers are there. Nothing is impossible.

> *The world makes way for those who know where they are going.*
>
> Ralph Waldo Emerson

Take some time and review what you have listed here and what you had written in Part I of this book. Are you exercising your rights as defined in Discipline #1? Did you consider and address some of the ineffective habits you listed in Discipline # 3? Do you see a connection with your values that you identified in Discipline # 4? Are you following the retirement plans that you have listed in Discipline #5? And will your dreams lead you to become the person you hope to be remembered as? Are your long-range dreams an extension of your short-range ones?

You should answer "Yes" to these questions. If not, ask yourself why, and make the necessary adjustments before you move on.

With this information now down on paper, do you sense a purpose to your life? You can define that purpose in three categories: what you want *to be*, what you want *to do*, and what you want *to have*.

What I would like to be:

_____

_____

_____

_____

_____

What I would like to do:

_____

_____

_____

_____

_____

Online for Life

What I would like to have:

_____

_____

_____

_____

_____

Now, using this information, draft an overall mission statement that describes your purpose. Think about what you are truly out to accomplish in life.

_____

_____

_____

_____

_____

_____

_____

Carry this statement with you. Refer to it often and make changes to it as you go.

Summary ⌒

Discipline # 6: Group, Categorize and Prioritize

Group dreams into categories by title.

Prioritize dreams and categories. Place them into time periods.

Compare your dreams with the exercises you completed in the first five disciplines. The picture of yourself that you developed in Part I should be consistent with your most important dreams.

Define your purpose: what do you want to be, do and have?

Thought space

_____

_____

_____

_____

_____

_____

_____

_____

_____

_____

_____

_____

_____

_____

Online for Life

_____

_____

_____

_____

_____

_____

_____

_____

_____

_____

_____

_____

Discipline # 7
Identify What You Are Prepared
to Give in Exchange

Nothing happens by itself...it all will come your way, once you understand that you have to make it come your way, by your own exertions.

Ben Stein

You have the right to lunch when you pay for it. There is no free lunch. In other words, you can achieve all the dreams and desires that you listed in the previous chapter, but you must give something in exchange for them. They will not just happen. What price are you willing to pay to accomplish your dreams?

Expect to make changes in your life: in the way you spend your time, effort and money, and in your relationships, habits, education and career. It is best to be aware of these costs up front. This way you can avoid surprises, and obtain support from the people who will be affected by your plan. Follow this discipline to identify and accept those costs of change.

One year each member of my family wrote out five goals that they wanted to accomplish. The one goal we all had in common was to build our dream home on the Gatineau River. We considered the costs of realizing this dream. The first cost would be the sale of our existing home. Would we get the price we wanted? Then, we would have to spend the time and effort to find the financing, architect and contractors for our new home. This would be at the cost of personal, family and career time. Then, where would we live during the period of construction? Could we live in the boathouse on our building site? We would save rent money, but there would be a comfort cost to living in that small, unheated space.

We concluded that, in order to build the house of our dreams, we were prepared to take a small financial loss on the sale of our existing home, give up personal, family and business time, and live under difficult conditions that could affect our relationships.

We lived with the costs and accomplished our dream. We are thankful that we were aware of those costs before we chose to begin. Knowing the costs in advance, and being prepared to pay the price, eliminated most stress and allowed us to succeed. It is better to be prepared than surprised.

Identify the costs associated with each priority time-period dream on the following pages. Are you prepared to pay the price to live your dreams? If not, consider your options.

Now it is your turn to accomplish your dream. Start with the top-priority dream you chose to achieve within the next three to six months.

Dream: _____

_____

In order to accomplish this dream I realize that there will be costs. The costs will be:

Time: _____

_____

The 12 Disciplines for Living Your Dreams

Effort: _____

_____

Relationships: _____

_____

Habits: _____

_____

Career: _____

_____

Education: _____

_____

Money: _____

_____

Other: _____

_____

Repeat the process for the top-priority dream you chose to achieve within the next twelve months.

Dream: _____

_____

In order to accomplish this dream I realize that there will be costs. The costs will be:

Time: _____

_____

Effort: _____
_____

Relationships: _____
_____

Habits: _____
_____

Career: _____
_____

Education: _____
_____

Money: _____
_____

Other: _____
_____

Repeat the process for the top-priority dream you chose to achieve within the next three to five years.

Dream: _____
_____

In order to accomplish this dream I realize that there will be costs. The costs will be:

Time: _____
_____

The 12 Disciplines for Living Your Dreams

Effort: _____

_____

Relationships: _____

_____

Habits: _____

_____

Career: _____

_____

Education: _____

_____

Money: _____

_____

Other: _____

_____

Repeat the process for the top-priority dream you chose to achieve within your lifetime.

Dream: _____

_____

In order to accomplish this dream I realize that there will be costs. The costs will be:

Time: _____

_____

Online for Life

Effort: _____
_____

Relationships: _____
_____

Habits: _____
_____

Career: _____
_____

Education: _____
_____

Money: _____
_____

Other: _____
_____

Are you prepared to pay the price? If so, move forward.
If not, consider your options.

Summary ⌒

Discipline # 7: Identify What You Are Prepared to Give in Exchange

You can have all your dreams and desires, but you must give something in exchange for them.

Expect to make changes in your life: in the way you spend your time, effort and money, and in your relationships, habits, education and career.

Thought space

_____

_____

_____

_____

_____

_____

_____

_____

_____

_____

_____

_____

_____

_____

Online for Life

Discipline # 8
Create a Goal Logbook

Success is the progressive realization of worthwhile goals.

Earl Nightingale

You have now conceived your dreams. Because you can see them in your mind's eye, it is very possible that you will live them. Visualizing your dreams is the first step to making them a reality. When you believe in your dreams, nothing but self-imposed limitations will stop you from achieving them.

In this discipline you will create a goal logbook. For each goal, you will identify possible obstacles, the skills and behavior you will employ, and people and groups who may be of assistance to you. You will develop a step-by-step action plan with milestone dates.

Your first step is to define your dreams as goals. A goal is a specific and measurable result that must be achieved within specified time, resource and cost constraints. A goal is an end, a result, and not just a task to be performed. It describes the condition we want to achieve. Our goals guide our actions and help us plan at work and at home. When we focus on our goals, long- and short-range, our present is determined by our future...not our past.

Visualize your first goal. Clearly understand your destination. Now the steps you take will all be in the right direction. You can examine each part of your life in the context of what really matters to you. Your goals are an extension of your values.

Goal setting is the process you use to select, define and put into operation the expectations that you have for yourself.

Why set goals? What's in it for you?

1. Goal setting focuses your efforts and improves your direction in life.
2. Goal setting causes you to set priorities and become more organized.
3. Goal setting turns your wishful thinking into reality.
4. Goal setting points out to you your successes as you achieve them, motivating you on to further success.
5. Goal setting can improve your self-esteem.
6. Goal setting makes you responsible for your own life. It causes you to define your own value system.
7. Goal setting makes you aware of your strengths, which you can use to overcome obstacles and solve problems.
8. Goal setting points out your weaknesses. You can begin setting new goals to improve in those areas and turn them into strengths.

Record keeping is important. Writing down your goals and action plans represents a commitment. Otherwise your dreams are merely wishful thinking. You can reread and visualize written goals. They are credible and legitimate. They live and lead you onward. When you write you have begun to act. Inertia is gone. You sense accomplishment already.

How should you phrase your goals? Goals must be S.M.A.R.T.— **S**pecific, **M**easurable, **A**ttainable, **R**elevant and **T**rackable to a Timetable. Let's look at each of these elements in detail.

1. Goals must be *specific*. "Happiness" or "success" are too vague. Ask yourself: What exactly do I want to do, be or have? For example, let's say you are getting too close to weighing 200 pounds and you want to reduce to 185 pounds within six months. You could write: In order to be healthier and more energetic, I will lose 14 pounds within the next six months, starting today, and maintain a weight of 185 pounds from that point on.

2. Is your goal *measurable*? How will you know you obtained your goal?

3. Is it *attainable*? Give yourself a chance to succeed. Take little steps and succeed. Success breeds success.

4. Is it *relevant*? Would the attainment of the goal be worthwhile to you? Before you can answer this question you need to know what kind of life you want.

5. Is there a way of *tracking* your performance on a timetable? How do you know you are getting closer to your goal? Select dates when you will measure your progress against the milestones in your plan. You will either reaffirm that you are on track or make adjustments.

Consider the following as you set each goal:

A. Is this goal really mine? Am I doing this for myself or somebody else? If you are doing it for somebody else, you are not living a life of *your* choosing.

B. Is it morally right and fair?

C. Are my short-range goals consistent with my long-range goals? Keep in mind where you want to be 10 to 20 years from now.

D. Can I commit myself to complete the project? If not, don't set yourself up for failure and disappointment. Save the goal for a time in your life when you can commit to make the effort.

E. Can I visualize myself reaching this goal? If you can't see it, it won't happen. Henry Ford said it best, "Whether you think you can or you think you can't, you're absolutely right."

Now start writing in your goal logbook. Describe in detail each goal, the methods you will use to attain it, and the dated milestones on the road to accomplishment. You will find logbook pages for three goals at the end of this chapter. You can complete the exercise on blank sheets of paper.

State the Goal

> *When you know what your specific objectives are concerning your distant, immediate and intermediate goals, you will be more apt to recognize that which will help you achieve them.*
>
> W. Clement Stone

Go back and review your top-priority dreams and your mission statement. Take a moment now and write out one of your short-range goals on a logbook page at the end of this chapter. Then do the same for a medium-range goal and a long-range goal. You will find a form for each one.

Once you have it written out, review it to see if the goal is S.M.A.R.T. Remember, to be S.M.A.R.T. it must be specific (well defined or described) measurable, attainable, realistic and trackable (to a specific date).

I remember doing a workshop and a participant had the following goal: "to build a chalet by May." I asked if she felt it was S.M.A.R.T.? The group started to analyze her goal. They all started to ask her questions about size, exterior and interior finish, location and more. Before long that goal was revised to: to build and move into a 1,500 square-meter luxury post and beam chalet featuring hardwood floors, low maintenance and a southern exposure towards the ski hills at Mont Tremblant, Quebec by May 30, 2000. It could have been even more specific, but this made the goal much clearer.

Be as descriptive as possible. Understand or define the meaning of each word used. You want to create as clear a picture as you possibly can in as few words as possible.

Date for Completion

> *From the first day in hospital I had set myself goals. I had promised myself I would be out of that Stryker bed for my birthday, August 26, and I was.*
>
> Rick Hansen

The next step is to add a completion date for each of your goals. Be the master of those dates, not the slave. Don't abandon your goals, just change the deadlines if you have to. Self-motivation and personal leadership include the ability to distinguish between defeat and setback.

Turn to your logbook pages now and write in a realistic deadline for each of your goals. You will lay out the milestones toward these dates later in your action plan.

Outcomes

> *Chance favors the prepared mind.*
>
> Louis Pasteur

The outcome is the result you want, expressed in detail. State your outcomes in positive, sensory-based terms: the sights, sounds and feelings you want to experience. For example, look at the weight-reduction goal: "Within six months, I will weigh 185 pounds." I *see* myself slimmer, my clothes fit better, and I am more attractive. I *hear* the opening of the storage box of clothes that had gotten too tight, people giving me compliments on my weight, saying how good I look and asking me how I did it. I *feel* energized, healthy and active.

Take a few moments now and imagine four things you will see, hear and feel when you have completed your goal. Write them in the logbook.

Possible Obstacles

Obstacles are those frightful things you see when you take your eyes off your goal.

Henry Ford

The next task is to identify the obstacles that could stand in your way. What events or circumstances might make it difficult to reach your goal? How will you handle those roadblocks? It is better to identify them now and have alternate plans ready than to be caught by surprise. Be ready.

Take the time now to list all the obstacles that you might encounter. Once you have done this for each of your goals, go back and prepare your contingency plans. "If this happened, I would…" Be ready.

Allow me to share an incident that occurred in my life that led me to identifying obstacles and contingency plans in advance on all of my goals.

Just before turning thirty years old, I decided to leave the security of the corporate world to go into business for myself selling residential lots in West Quebec. This was influenced by the level of success I was experiencing in selling land there for my existing employer, Canada's second largest land developer at the time.

Both of Canada's largest land developers and builders were getting out of the new-house construction market in the early 1980s. Real estate just wasn't selling. Interest rates were at an all-time high and a separatist government was in power in Quebec.

While employed with one of the developers, I was responsible for over 10,000 acres of commercial, industrial and residential land in the National Capital Region. I also sold a lot of their land in Aylmer and Gatineau, Quebec. I was the only one selling at the time. It got to the point where licensed real estate agents reported me to the Quebec Real Estate

Board. I was investigated and learned a lot about what is allowed and what is not. The conclusion was that as long as I was selling land for a developer, I didn't need a real estate license.

Within weeks Canada's largest land developer approached me to ask if I would consider selling for them too. They suggested I leave and take on a contract with my existing employer and with them. I always wanted to be in business for myself and I figured that this would be the time, as we only had one young child. I approached my employer and obtained their support.

Immediately I started on a plan. The plan was to prepare the lots for a mass sale six weeks before an upcoming provincial election. During the period before, I had the lots backhoed, picketed and signed with lot numbers, dimensions and phone numbers.

Finally, the time arrived. I expected big results, and being the proactive guy that I am, I started to investigate commercial land development opportunities. The marketing kicked in, as did the support from the local media. Within five days, I had sold over 100 individual lots and earned just over $80,000 in commissions. Not a bad week after being in business for only six months.

Expecting this to happen, I had exercised an option to purchase some commercial land and went to work on it immediately. I was creating a major tourist attraction, and spent $100,000 within the next twenty days preparing the site.

By the time thirty days rolled around, suppliers were looking for money. I was wondering what happened to mine. I called the office of Canada's largest land developer. There was no answer. I drove into town and visited their office only to learn that it was closed down and everyone I knew had been let go. I would have to direct my inquiries to a vice-president located in head office in Toronto.

Before long, I met with that VP. After hearing me out, he said he liked me and would give me $5,000. Otherwise, go play in the traffic. He felt he wasn't obliged to pay me because I was not a licensed real estate agent. I could not believe what he was saying. I decided to refuse his offer and seek legal advise, based on the experience I gained from being previously investigated.

Because of a very simple obstacle that could have been identified in advance (with a contingency plan put in place) my "success" became a nightmare.

All five goals that were well in line for accomplishment experienced a major setback. First, I was obliged to pay my suppliers. I went to the local bank and borrowed $10,000 at a 22 percent interest rate. In the end I had borrowed ten $10,000 loans at 22 percent interest. My mortgage came up for renewal at 19% and my lawyer advised me to give him $25,000 up front for court costs or move out of our dream home and into an apartment in Ottawa to avoid Ontario Supreme Court costs. That hurt the most. My wife Joan was pregnant with our second child and was looking forward to raising our children at home. We moved out, rented out our home and found an apartment in town.

It wasn't long after that I had no choice but to close down the business I had started. I was now in significant debt. Fortunately I landed a job and slowly began to rebuild. Within three years, Canada's largest land developer settled out of court and I secured all monies due to me. I got myself back on my feet again, and ended up in a better position because of the experience.

However, there is no need to go through what I went through. If I had only addressed one possible obstacle: what if they decide not to pay me?

Had I even thought of it, I would have waited for the money to be in my hands before proceeding into further investment. That would have been my contingency plan.

Mind you, I do have a "do it now" attitude and don't usually take the time to think about everything that can go wrong. I learn by doing and adjusting as need be. You don't want to think about obstacles for too long, because it will delay you in your actions. Identify the most obvious and potentially most serious ones that come to mind and move on.

Contingency Plans

Success comes to those who set goals and pursue them regardless of obstacles and disappointments.

Napoleon Hill

Based on the possible obstacles you have identified, what can you do in advance to prepare? If that obstacle caught you by surprise it could knock you down. If you have a contingency plan, you will stand tall and realize it as just a bump along the road to success. You implement your contingency plan and move on. You just saved yourself two steps in the process—one being knocked down and the other getting back up. Don't let it take three years out of your life as it did to me.

Take the time now to identify some possible contingency plans to obstacles you identified earlier.

Skills and Behaviors Required

Almost every goal you set for yourself involves learning. The ability to learn what you need to know, in a hurry, is the basic tool for getting what you want.

Joyce Brothers

What skills will you require for you to achieve your goal? How, where and when will you learn those skills?

Behavior can be defined as the way you conduct yourself. Will you need to change your behavior in order to put your skills into action?

For example, when we laid out our goal to build our dream home, I needed to acquire some design and construction skills. Not so much the "to do" skills but rather an understanding of them in order to negotiate and inspect the hired skills. So I made it a goal to take a course on building your own home, which turned out to be invaluable.

I developed my behaviors, too. I researched designs and materials. I read up on things, spoke to many contractors, and made sure I was on top of everything. I learned how to accept criticism and provide constructive feedback to the tradesmen, maintain a positive attitude and to persist until the job got done.

People, Groups or Resources Required

> *In order to reach your ultimate goal, you must form a group of people with ambitions like your own, but differing in specialized knowledge. Together, the group can solve problems that no one person alone could solve.*
>
> Napoleon Hill

You can accomplish only so much on your own. You can achieve much more by calling on the help of different people, groups or resources. Regardless of your goal, you will attain it with much less difficulty if you ally yourself with others. Some people create mastermind groups, others create an advisory board, others consult with their friends and families, while others benefit from being members of an association. It is through others that we sometimes get our best ideas. The best results come from an organized effort of two or more people working towards a definite outcome.

What individuals or groups of people could help you? What resources can you call on? List them now.

_____

_____

_____

_____

For example, while completing the log for my goal to become a speaker, I wanted to become part of a professional speaking association, so I joined the Canadian Association of Professional Speakers. I felt I needed an individual to help fast-track me into the business, internationally. The timing was right and I found Denis Cauvier, right in my own town. When I looked for a speech coach to provide me with constructive feedback, I found Velma Latmore, a person who has dedicated her life to effective communications through Toastmasters. I also needed resource material, so I reorganized my office and got out all the books that had inspired me over the years. I began researching using the Internet and visiting bookstores regularly.

Action Plan

> *Say three times "This one thing I do", emphasizing the word one. One step at a time will get you there much more surely than haphazardly leaping and jumping. It is the steady pace, the consistent speed that leads the most efficient start to your destination.*
>
> Dr. Norman Vincent Peale

An action plan is a step-by-step outline of the tasks that lead to the achievement of a goal. Treat each action step as a sub-goal.

What do you need to do to turn your goals into reality? Establish a logical sequence of steps. Prioritize them and place a target date for accomplishment beside each activity. By dating each step along the way you can monitor and measure your progress and reward yourself accordingly.

Acknowledge the events beyond your control upon which goal results depend. Identify the areas where you will co-ordinate your actions with other people, in order to get the support you need, when you need it.

Identifying the actions you need to take, and the schedule for those actions, makes all the difference between a wish and a realistic, achievable goal. The main objective is to set up your action plan in a way that guarantees you success. By this, I mean create an action plan that is full of little steps at a time so that you can experience success along the way.

Too many people just identify gigantic steps. Steps that turn out to be unrealistic or unachievable in the time frames allocated. They soon sense that they can't do it and then give up. Don't do that to yourself.

Create an action plan that is set up for success. Little steps at a time. Experience your success on a daily basis. It is like a saying I once heard: You cannot eat an elephant at one time, it will take many days and many bites to eat it all. You can't realize your tomorrow's dream without first taking a small step forward today towards its realization.

For example, 20 years ago I laid out a three-phase action plan to build a waterfront home for my family. The first phase was to learn about the local real estate. Over the years I acquired a good understanding of land, and when river-front properties finally became available I found the perfect lot.

The next phase was to pay off and prepare the land. Over a period of five years I cleared the trees, put in the driveway, fixed the shoreline, built a boathouse, and put in a septic bed, a flower garden and grass. The property was ready. The only thing missing was the house.

The third and concluding phase was to design the house, to sell our old home, acquire the financing and build. One step at a time, we accomplished a dream that went back 20 years.

Take the time now to list all the necessary steps to accomplish each of your goals. Use extra paper if you need it. This is the most important stage in creating your goal logbook. Take the time to list everything that comes to mind. When you are done, review your list and identify the steps in order of priority. Spend a lot of time in this area before moving on. Identify everything right down to the little steps and set yourself up for success.

Methods of Monitoring and Measuring Progress

Goals are not only absolutely necessary to motivate us. They are essential to really keep us alive.

Robert H. Schuller

Knowing how you're doing will motivate you to keep going. How will you monitor your behavior and measure your progress? Think of some ways in which you can do this on an ongoing basis. Monitoring will allow you to recognize your progress and reward yourself accordingly. It will also warn you to take corrective action should you find you are not following your plan.

In Discipline #11, I will share with you a simple form of monitoring and measuring. But start to think about it now. How can you make sure you are on track? What sort of measurements can you take regularly? Fill in that part of your logbook pages now.

The Reward (What's in it for me?)

> *I feel the greatest reward for doing is the opportunity to do more.*
>
> Jonas Salk

How are you going to reward yourself when you accomplish your goal? You deserve something besides the achievement of that goal. Visualize the rewards you'll give yourself. Also, decide how you can pay yourself along the way. It will be easier to keep up the good work when you periodically reward yourself.

What are the things you really enjoy? Plan to treat yourself to some of these things after you complete each action step. This way you will practice discipline—doing what you have to do even when you don't want to—and accomplish your goals at the same time. Remember that action that gets rewarded gets repeated.

For example, I like to play golf with clients on Friday afternoons. I usually take some time on Sunday evenings to plan out my week in relation to my monthly goals. I identify the times during the week where I have family and business commitments, and then I fill in my schedule with activities that will help me reach my goals for that month. Before long my schedule is full. By the time Friday rolls around, I either reward myself by playing golf, because I did everything I indicated that I would, or I punish myself and stay in the office and do everything that I didn't do.

Imagine if I rewarded myself for something I indicated that I would do but then didn't do. Do you think I would have a good game of golf? I don't think so. I would be feeling kind of guilty. However, imagine how well I would play golf, and how much more I would enjoy the game, if it were a reward for doing what I indicated to myself that I would do.

You can use dinners, movies, vacations, clothes, events or whatever you enjoy as a reward. Tie the required disciplines to something you really enjoy and treat them as a reward for doing what you indicated you would do. Stop treating yourself to these enjoyments for absolutely no reason, and you will soon be a master of discipline.

Discipline is the key. Discipline is a commitment to yourself to do what you have to do, even when you don't want to do it. As discipline gets recognized and rewarded it gets repeated and becomes a matter of habit.

Commitment

> *There is not much use climbing the ladder part way.*
> *People who succeed have the single-minded devotion to*
> *their goal that is best described as total commitment.*
> *They have the ability and desire to work to top capacity.*
>
> Joyce Brothers

This is where you make a commitment to yourself. This is such an important step that I have dedicated Discipline #9 to it. Before you sign your goal logbook, I suggest you read Discipline #9.

Short-range Goal

The date I created this log: _____

The last time I updated it:_____

State the goal _____
_____
_____

Date for completion _____

Outcome _____
_____
_____

What will I see when I get there?
1. _____
2. _____
3. _____
4. _____

What sounds will I hear?
1. _____
2. _____
3. _____
4. _____

What will I feel?

1. _____
2. _____
3. _____
4. _____

Possible obstacles _____
_____
_____
_____
_____

Contingency plans_____
_____
_____
_____
_____

Skills and behaviors required
_____
_____
_____
_____

People, groups or resources required
_____
_____
_____
_____

Action Plan with Dates

Action # _____

Start: _____ *Finish:* _____

Action # _____

Start: _____ *Finish:* _____

Action # _____

Start: _____ *Finish:* _____

Action # _____

Start: _____ *Finish:* _____

Action # _____

Start: _____ *Finish:* _____

Action # _____

Start: _____ *Finish:* _____

Action # _____

Start: _____ *Finish:* _____

Action # _____

Start: _____ *Finish:* _____

Action # _____

Start: _____ *Finish:* _____

Action # _____

Start: _____ *Finish:* _____

Action # _____

Start: _____ *Finish:* _____

Action # _____

Start: _____ *Finish:* _____

Action # _____

Start: _____ *Finish:* _____

Action # _____

Start: _____ *Finish:* _____

Action # _____

Start: _____ *Finish:* _____

Methods of monitoring and measuring progress

_____

_____

_____

_____

The reward (What's in it for me?)

_____

_____

_____

_____

Commitment

I commit myself to accomplish this goal by the completion date on the first page of the goal logbook, by implementing each action outlined within the time frames indicated.

Signature: _____ Today's Date: _____

The 12 Disciplines for Living Your Dreams

Medium-range Goal

The date I created this log: _____

The last time I updated it: _____

State the goal _____
_____
_____

Date for completion _____

Outcome _____
_____
_____

What will I see when I get there?

1. _____
2. _____
3. _____
4. _____

What sounds will I hear?

1. _____
2. _____
3. _____
4. _____

What will I feel?

1. _____

2. _____

3. _____

4. _____

Possible obstacles _____

_____

_____

_____

_____

Contingency plans_____

_____

_____

_____

_____

Skills and behaviors required

_____

_____

_____

_____

People, groups or resources required

_____

_____

_____

_____

Action Plan with Dates

Action # _____

Start: _____   *Finish:* _____

Action # _____

Start: _____   *Finish:* _____

Action # _____

Start: _____   *Finish:* _____

Action # _____

Start: _____   *Finish:* _____

Action # _____

Start: _____   *Finish:* _____

Action # _____

Start: _____   *Finish:* _____

Action # _____

Start: _____   *Finish:* _____

Action # _____

Start: _____   *Finish:* _____

Action # _____

Start: _____   *Finish:* _____

Action # _____

Start: _____   *Finish:* _____

Action # _____

Start: _____   *Finish:* _____

Action # _____

Start: _____   *Finish:* _____

Action # _____

Start: _____   *Finish:* _____

Action # _____

Start: _____   *Finish:* _____

Methods of monitoring and measuring progress

_____

_____

_____

_____

The reward (What's in it for me?)

_____

_____

_____

_____

Commitment

I commit myself to accomplish this goal by the completion date on the first page of the goal logbook, by implementing each action outlined within the time frames indicated.

Signature: _____ Today's Date: _____

The 12 Disciplines for Living Your Dreams

Long-range Goal

The date I created this log: _____

The last time I updated it: _____

State the goal _____
_____
_____

Date for completion _____

Outcome _____
_____
_____

What will I see when I get there?
1. _____
2. _____
3. _____
4. _____

What sounds will I hear?
1. _____
2. _____
3. _____
4. _____

What will I feel?

1. _____
2. _____
3. _____
4. _____

Possible obstacles _____

_____
_____
_____
_____

Contingency plans_____

_____
_____
_____
_____

Skills and behaviors required

_____
_____
_____
_____

People, groups or resources required

_____
_____
_____
_____

Action Plan with Dates

Action # _____

Start: _____ *Finish:* _____

Action # _____

Start: _____ *Finish:* _____

Action # _____

Start: _____ *Finish:* _____

Action # _____

Start: _____ *Finish:* _____

Action # _____

Start: _____ *Finish:* _____

Action # _____

Start: _____ *Finish:* _____

Action # _____

Start: _____ *Finish:* _____

Action # _____

Start: _____ *Finish:* _____

Action # _____

Start: _____ *Finish:* _____

Action # _____

Start: _____ *Finish:* _____

Action # _____

Start: _____ *Finish:* _____

Action # _____

Start: _____ *Finish:* _____

Action # _____

Start: _____ *Finish:* _____

Action # _____

Start: _____ *Finish:* _____

Methods of monitoring and measuring progress

_____

_____

_____

_____

The reward (What's in it for me?)

_____

_____

_____

_____

Commitment

I commit myself to accomplish this goal by the completion date on the first page of the goal logbook, by implementing each action outlined within the time frames indicated.

Signature: _____

Date: _____

Summary ⌒

Discipline # 8: Create a Goal Logbook

A goal is an end, a result, not just a task to be performed. It describes the condition you want to achieve.

Goals are an extension of your values.

Goals must be S.M.A.R.T.—Specific, Measurable, Attainable, Relevant and Trackable to a Timetable.

Ask yourself: Is this goal really mine? Is it morally right and fair? Are my short-range goals consistent with my long-range goals? Can I commit myself to complete the project? Can I visualize myself reaching this goal?

Create a goal logbook and address each of the following areas:

- State the goal, date for completion and outcomes expressed in sensory-based terms: the sights, sounds and feelings you want to experience.

- Identify obstacles you might meet, develop the contingency plans to overcome those possible obstacles, identify the skills and behaviors you'll need, and the people, groups or resources you can call on for help.

- Develop a detailed step-by-step success-oriented action plan with start and finish dates, and with a method of monitoring and measuring your progress.

- Create a system to recognize and reward yourself for doing what you indicated you would do along the way.

- Finally, make a commitment to yourself to follow through and do what you have to do.

Thought space

_____
_____
_____
_____
_____
_____
_____
_____
_____
_____
_____
_____
_____
_____
_____

Discipline # 9
Commit to Your Action Plan

Always bear in mind that your own resolution to succeed is more important than any one thing.

Abraham Lincoln

Commitment: an agreement or pledge to do something in the future.

You have identified everything relating to the accomplishment of a goal. You've identified possible obstacles and are prepared for the "worst-case scenario." "If only" doesn't exist. Blaming others is a thing of the past.

To succeed you must discipline yourself and do what you have to do, even when you don't want to. Are you serious about accomplishing the goals you just outlined? Are you committed to following through? If you are, sign the pledge at the bottom of your goal logbook sheets.

Pledge yourself to your course of action and take on the complete responsibility to "make it happen." There are no more excuses. This is no longer "I hope." This is putting one foot ahead of the other and doing it. You are now making the biggest commitment you will ever make—a commitment to yourself.

Online for Life

Do you make New Year's resolutions? Do you manage to stick to them? If so, congratulations! You are part of a small and exceptional group. Most people give up on their "resolutions" within two to three weeks.

We respect, and usually follow through on, our commitments to others. When it comes to commitments to ourselves, though, we often allow external influences to win. We give in. And to make it worse, we tend to give in just under the 21-day mark when the habit could be broken, or the commitment could become habit. Rather than recognizing the success we had while trying to keep the resolution, we dwell on the "what if I can't do it?"

Of all commitments, the ones you make to yourself are the most important to respect. If you can't keep a commitment to yourself, you can't succeed.

To commit to something is to take a risk. You must loosen your hold on what you are certain of, and reach for the unknown that you believe is better than what you have. It's natural to be afraid when you take a risk. You are venturing into the unknown. But if you don't take risks you will live a life without growth. You will have to give up something in order to move ahead, but avoiding risks is the surest way of losing.

You can succeed if your willingness to leap overpowers your concern about what could happen if you fail. Avoid the regret of looking back on a life of opportunities not taken. Take the chance and commit to accomplishing your dreams.

> *I don't know when to stop. When I make a commitment,*
> *it is to the end.*
>
> James Garner

You are making a commitment to yourself to follow through on the action plans you outlined in the previous discipline. Go back and review them. Are your actions broken down into achievable steps? Did you give yourself enough time to accomplish each step? Have you set yourself up for success? If not, make the necessary adjustments. You want to succeed!

Be aware of your daily progress, because success breeds success. Discipline yourself and do whatever you have to do for at least the next 21 to 30 days, no matter what. Get yourself into a good habit.

If you are ready to commit now, sign your action plans and pledge yourself to action. Don't ever look back.

Summary

Discipline # 9: Commit to Your Action Plan

Commitment: an agreement or pledge to do something in the future.

You have to pledge yourself to your course of action, taking on the complete responsibility to "make it happen."

Of all commitments, the ones you make to yourself are the most important to respect.

To commit to something is to take a risk.

You can succeed if your willingness to leap overpowers your concern about what could happen if you fail.

Avoid the regret of looking back on a life of opportunities not taken.

Discipline yourself and do whatever you have to do for at least the next 21 to 30 days, no matter what.

Thought space

_____

_____

_____

_____

_____

_____

_____

_____

_____

_____

_____

Discipline # 10
Be Action Oriented

There is nothing brilliant nor outstanding in my record, except perhaps this one thing: I do the things that I believe ought to be done...and when I make up my mind to do a thing, I act!

Theodore Roosevelt

This is where the magic begins. By having a focus, and taking those steps-to-success daily, you start to feel good about yourself and your accomplishments. You are in control of your life and your attitude. You wake up each morning thankful for another day, with that great feeling that today is going to be worthwhile, rain or shine. Why? Because you are going to do something today to bring your dream a little step closer to reality, and you are going to congratulate yourself for having done it.

It all begins by becoming action oriented. You need a "do it now" attitude. The first two letters of goal are *go*. Now is the time to get going. "Do not tell the world what you can do—show it!"

(If you have completed all the previous exercises, you will find this discipline easy. You have demonstrated that you already appreciate the value of action.)

Avoid procrastination. Procrastination is the process of habitually putting things off. It is tempting to make excuses…"I don't have the time," "I think they said they were going to be in meetings all day, so I didn't call," "This could take forever; I'll do it when I have a spare day."

Procrastination will cause you to miss deadlines, leading to lost opportunities and income, lower productivity and wasted time. It will lower your motivation, heighten your stress and generate frustration and anger. Is this the way you want to live?

Take control of your life now! Reverse the procrastination habit by being as clever about completing things as you have been about putting them off. Don't expect to find time to achieve your goals. The only way to get time is to make time. Start by committing to a do-it-now mentality.

A do-it-now attitude makes you a self-starter—a person who can recognize a need and take appropriate action without waiting to be told to. As a self-starter you will avoid the pressure, frustration and anxiety that come from having others tell you what and how to do things. You exercise your creativity in solving problems and doing work. As a result, you are more productive. You take maximum advantage of every opportunity, your sense of timing sharpening. You seldom miss something you want because of being late. Your services become more eagerly sought-after.

This type of do-it-now attitude will also help you overcome your resistance to dealing with unpleasant tasks. Don't delay your gratification by delaying the unpleasant tasks. By tackling them first, you get them over with and can get on with the more pleasant things in life.

With an action-oriented, do-it-now attitude you get more out of your day. When you complete the unpleasant or hard jobs first and you act on the big tasks, little bites at a time, you'll trim your anxiety and stress load while gaining self-respect and self-confidence. After you exert this type of discipline long enough, you will establish a routine and make a new habit. Human behavior studies suggest that if you do something every day for 30 days, it will become a habit. Be consciously action oriented for the next 30 days and you will master procrastination.

Here are some action-oriented techniques to apply each day.

Determine your most productive time of the day and dedicate it to "I" time. "I" time is for you to do whatever you have to do that will bring you closer to achieving your goals. It may be as simple as visualizing the accomplishment of your goals or doing what you have to do, for you. The point is to dedicate the most productive time for the most important person in the world.

You have already set your goals and action plans and have prioritized the actions. Take your annual goals and break them down into months, weeks and, finally, days. Do the same with each day's activities. Break the large tasks down into small, manageable pieces. Try to accomplish some of these pieces each day. Before long you will have accomplished a large task.

End each day by writing a prioritized to-do list for the next day. At the end of each week and month do the same for the next week and month. Get organized. Use a daily planner. You will be better organized if you write down everything.

Clear your mind of clutter. Solve problems while they are small. Whatever you do, do it once, to the best of your ability, and move on. Question all tasks to make sure they are worthwhile. Do the worst or hardest jobs first.

Be decisive and remove time wasters, such as interruptions, from all of your activities. Remember to take care of yourself by exercising, watching your diet, and maintaining a balance in your life. And when evening comes and your next day's to-do list is written, celebrate. Action that gets rewarded gets repeated. Do this for 30 days and you will be transformed into an action-oriented, do-it-now person.

An action-oriented person is proactive. When you are proactive, you have initiative—you can see a need, figure out how to best satisfy it, determine the appropriate time to take the right action, and proceed.

When you are proactive, you lead. When you lead, you take control of yourself and get the things you want out of life.

Try using the visualization technique to help yourself become action oriented. When you set your goals you pictured something that you wanted to have, be or do. Everything we have or do is preceded by an image in our mind. Visualization is seeing the end result. It is a form of mental rehearsal. Through the use of imagination, what you see is what you will get.

Your vision of your goals must be clear. There is a difference between 'dreaming about having something in the future' and 'visualizing having it in the future.' The power to believe makes the difference. Visualizing implies a structured and disciplined view of what you are trying to accomplish. Through visualization you picture yourself already in possession of your goal. By visualizing you look at your goal from many different viewpoints. By examining your goal from all of the viewpoints, you see the situation clearly and can act on the aspects that will result in the greatest payback.

> *Go put your creed into your deed.*
> Ralph Waldo Emerson

Make this a daily discipline. Visualize to actualize your goals. Forget all your inhibitions. See things as you want them to be, not as they are. Take time to sit back, close your eyes, and see yourself accomplishing your goal. You are watching a movie based on the success that you have become. Focus your attention on the results. See yourself there. Feel the emotions. See the colors, the details; hear the sounds.

If you form a clear and detailed picture of your future, ways and means of getting it will be revealed to you. Keep focusing on what you want, not on how you will do it. The laws of nature will take over. The more you visualize, the more resources you will attract. Your vision will act as a magnet. It will attract people, events and circumstances to it. It is a self-fulfilling prophecy.

And when you're having a difficult moment during the day, take the time to visualize the accomplishment of your goal. It will refocus and relax you, and the issue of the moment will matter less. The major incident of today will probably be insignificant in the future. Don't trip over molehills.

Try visualizing right now. Project yourself six months into the future. Select one of your short-range goals. Now get comfortable and close your eyes. See yourself accomplishing your goal. You are now successfully there. You made it, you're living and breathing it. Use your imagination. See all the details, hear the sounds, feel the emotions, and celebrate. Visualize this for the next five minutes. Focus on the success.

I recommend that you get into the habit of doing this daily. Your enthusiastic attitude about your vision will not only keep you motivated, it will get others excited about your dream.

Just as thoughts can control feelings and feelings control behavior, the reverse is also true. If you change your behavior you can change your feelings and ultimately your thoughts. It is not how you feel that determines how you act, it is how you act that determines how you feel. For example, if you pull your shoulders back, lift your head high, force yourself to smile and cheerfully greet others, you will find your mood changing.

The same process applies to self-talk. Feed your mind negative thoughts and it will produce negative actions. Feed your mind positive, confident information and your mind will react in kind. You cannot completely control the circumstances around you, but you can control what you say to yourself and how you think.

These techniques, all easy to do, are the daily steps that will lead you to success. Each success breeds success. There will be obstacles along the way, and when they get in your way, be ready for them. You must persist. Stick to it. You will get things done, and meet your objectives and goals. Keep in mind that often when we are ready to quit, success lies just around the corner. Don't ever give up on taking action. Make your dreams happen!

Summary

Discipline # 10: Be Action-Oriented

This is where the magic begins.

You need a "do it now" attitude, so don't procrastinate!

Don't expect to *find* time to achieve your goals; instead, *make* the time.

Determine your most productive time of the day and dedicate it to the most important person in the world. This is "I" time.

Deal with the unpleasant, large or hard tasks first.

Create a prioritized to-do list daily, weekly and monthly.

Accomplish some piece of a major objective daily.

Remove time wasters. Take care of yourself with exercise, a healthy diet, and a balanced life.

Every day, visualize in detail the end result.

Change your behavior and you can change your feelings and ultimately your thoughts.

Control what you say to yourself and how you think.

Success breeds success.

Don't ever give up on taking action. Make your dream happen!

Thought space

_____

_____

_____

_____

_____

_____

_____

Discipline # 11
Monitor and Measure Your Progress

We are what we repeatedly do. Excellence, then, is not an act, but a habit.

Aristotle

Are you doing what you set out to do? If so, are you rewarding yourself for your accomplishments? If not, are you revising your plan? Knowing how you're doing will motivate you to keep going and to make the necessary adjustments along the way. You will find the two charts at the end of this chapter helpful to monitor your actions and behavior.

Here's the way it works. You take the goal categories that you identified in Discipline #6, and on the Goal Chart write each category name in the column under the title "Goals." Then, on the line beside each category, write out the goals for each time period.

Although the chart shows time periods of Year 1, 3, 5 and long-term, you may use whatever time periods you prefer. I use a six-month period for my short-range goals. I use my birthday as the beginning of a new year. I use the three- and five-year columns for my medium-range goals and "long-term" for my retirement and whole-life goals.

The beauty of the Goal Chart is that it summarizes all the expectations and dreams that you intend to turn into reality. Your completed Goal Chart reminds you of what is truly important in your life. It reinforces your expectations and gives you a boost in down times. It helps you in your visualization process. It is your roadmap to your future.

Use this chart daily and you will no longer waste time sitting in traffic or waiting on someone. You will no longer get upset about the minor incidents in your day. Why will your attitude improve? Because you are reading your Goal Chart, reviewing your goals and visualizing their accomplishment. You are projecting your mind into a time of happiness and success by visualizing goal accomplishment. It's easy, fun and rewarding. "Your thoughts of today are your tomorrow."

My Goal Chart is with me at all times. I review it regularly, add to it as I go, and update it every six months, or as need be. My Goal Chart has kept me focused on what is important to me.

Take the time now and fill in your Goal Chart. Write down your categories and goals under the appropriate time periods. Fill in what you can now, and update it regularly.

> *The goal of yesterday will be the starting point of tomorrow.*
> Thomas Carlyle

The Monthly Monitor Chart provides you with a method to monitor your behavior and activity. Look first at "Activities." Across the top of the chart are the numbers 1 to 31. These are for each day of the month. Down the side of the chart is a list of daily activities. Check your daily progress in each activity for each goal. Fill in the chart each day. Place a check mark next to each activity that you carried out that day.

Are you doing what you set out to do? Are you really committed? The Monthly Monitor Chart will soon tell you. If you need to, adjust your goal to more chewable pieces. You may change, or add to, this list of daily activities.

Now look at "Goals" on the Monthly Monitor Chart. Here you will list your top three goals for that month. Under each goal you identify three daily actions toward the accomplishment of that goal. Review and monitor each of these every day.

Select three goals that you want to work on this month and list them under "Goals" on the Monthly Monitor Chart. Then identify three actions to take this month to help you accomplish each of those goals. Those actions could be something you'll repeat daily or weekly, or do once only. Write down what you think you can accomplish. Take time now to complete this section. (There are four sets of these charts located at the end of this chapter.)

The Goal Chart summarizes your short- and long-range goals, and the Monthly Monitor Chart details what you plan to do each day and month. Combined, they serve as a great tool. The charts will remind, discipline, guide, monitor and reward you. They will make you more aware of your behaviors, pointing out when you should make adjustments. They are my guide and can be yours too. Complete the charts and carry them with you at all times. Refer to them at least three times a day. Fill in the Monthly Monitor daily and revise it monthly. The effort will help you make your dreams your reality.

This chart has helped to direct my life. At the end of each month I review my accomplishments. One month I had a goal to spend more time with my family. At the end of the month I reviewed my Monthly Monitor Chart and noticed that for that goal I had only 7 of 31 days checked off. I asked myself if I was really serious about this goal, and what was I going to do about it?

When I looked back over that month, I realized that I had been traveling three weeks for my job. My job was important to me, but I concluded that time with my sons was more important. So I created a new goal for the next month: to find another job that would allow me to be at home in the evenings and spend less time on the road. Two months later I changed jobs and got what I wanted—more time at home with my family.

You too will experience the benefits of these charts if you use them regularly. I've been filling them in daily and revising them monthly since I created them five years ago. I recommend that you get yourself into the same habit.

The 12 Disciplines for Living Your Dreams

Goal Chart ™

GOAL CATEGORY	YEAR 1	YEAR 3	YEAR 4	LONG TERM

THE MONTHLY MONITOR CHART ™

ACTIVITIES	1	2	3	4	5	6	7	8	9	10	11	12	13	14	15	16	17	18	19	20	21	22	23	24	25	26	27	28	29	30	31
Goal Review																															
A.M.																															
Noon																															
P.M.																															
I recognize and praise																															
I visualize and use imaginery																															
I talk positively to myself																															
I am an empathetic listener																															
I am patient and I probe																															

Goal #1 _____
Actions 1. _____
2. _____
3. _____

Goal #2 _____
Actions 1. _____
2. _____
3. _____

Goal #3 _____
Actions 1. _____
2. _____
3. _____

Goal Chart ™

GOAL CATEGORY	YEAR 1	YEAR 3	YEAR 4	LONG TERM

THE MONTHLY MONITOR CHART ™

ACTIVITIES	1	2	3	4	5	6	7	8	9	10	11	12	13	14	15	16	17	18	19	20	21	22	23	24	25	26	27	28	29	30	31
Goal Review																															
A.M.																															
Noon																															
P.M.																															
I recognize and praise																															
I visualize and use imaginery																															
I talk positively to myself																															
I am an empathetic listener																															
I am patient and I probe																															

Goal #1 _____
Actions
1. _____
2. _____
3. _____

Goal #2 _____
Actions
1. _____
2. _____
3. _____

Goal #3 _____
Actions
1. _____
2. _____
3. _____

Goal Chart ™

GOAL CATEGORY	YEAR 1	YEAR 3	YEAR 4	LONG TERM

THE MONTHLY MONITOR CHART ™

ACTIVITIES	1	2	3	4	5	6	7	8	9	10	11	12	13	14	15	16	17	18	19	20	21	22	23	24	25	26	27	28	29	30	31
Goal Review A.M.																															
Noon																															
P.M.																															
I recognize and praise																															
I visualize and use imaginery																															
I talk positively to myself																															
I am an empathetic listener																															
I am patient and I probe																															

Goal #1 _____

Actions
1. _____
2. _____
3. _____

Goal #2 _____

Actions
1. _____
2. _____
3. _____

Goal #3 _____

Actions
1. _____
2. _____
3. _____

Goal Chart ™

GOAL CATEGORY	YEAR 1	YEAR 3	YEAR 4	LONG TERM

THE MONTHLY MONITOR CHART ™

ACTIVITIES	1	2	3	4	5	6	7	8	9	10	11	12	13	14	15	16	17	18	19	20	21	22	23	24	25	26	27	28	29	30	31
Goal Review																															
A.M.																															
Noon																															
P.M.																															
I recognize and praise																															
I visualize and use imaginery																															
I talk positively to myself																															
I am an empathetic listener																															
I am patient and I probe																															

Goal #1 _____
Actions 1. _____
2. _____
3. _____

Goal #2 _____
Actions 1. _____
2. _____
3. _____

Goal #3 _____
Actions 1. _____
2. _____
3. _____

Summary ⌒

Discipline # 11: Monitor and Measure Your Progress

Knowing how you're doing will motivate you to keep going and to make the necessary adjustments along the way.

The Goal Chart summarizes all the expectations and dreams that you intend to turn into reality.

The Monthly Monitor Chart provides you with a 31-day habit-forming process for monitoring and measuring your progress.

The charts remind, discipline, guide, monitor and reward you. They make you aware of your behaviors, pointing out where and when you should make adjustments.

Thought space

_____

_____

_____

_____

_____

_____

_____

_____

_____

_____

_____

_____

_____

_____

_____

_____
_____
_____
_____
_____
_____
_____
_____
_____
_____
_____
_____
_____
_____
_____
_____
_____
_____

Discipline # 12
Be Thankful

Reflect upon your present blessings, of which every man has plenty; not on your past misfortunes, of which all men have some.

Charles Dickens

We all want a lot out of life. You are now focused, disciplined and ready to move into action to have more. First, take inventory of what you have now.

What do you have to be thankful for?

_____

_____

_____

_____

_____

_____

Did you mention the natural world—the things we usually take for granted? Think. Compare yourself to others who are less fortunate, here at home or elsewhere in the world. What about those in hospitals and prisons? Do you have freedom? Any possessions to be thankful for? Do you have an income? What about the people in your life—anyone there to be thankful for? How is your life—your health, mind, body and spirit? Can you see, hear, taste, smell, and feel? Can you speak? Are you breathing?

We have so much to be thankful for, don't we? Take a moment and count your blessings.

We are so fortunate, yet we rarely take the time to smell the roses in our lives. This too is a daily discipline. Practicing thankfulness is about not taking life for granted. Greet the morning by being thankful for receiving another day. Think of the people who would have liked to have another day, but didn't, or those who are hanging on to life one day at a time. For all you know this could be the last day of *your* life. Be thankful that you are alive.

How will you respond if someone asks, "How are you today?" "Not bad, good, okay, so-so, tired, sore, better than yesterday." Is this you, or *was* this you? How should you respond? Write down your answers.

How are you?

_____

_____

_____

_____

_____

_____

Now that you have counted your blessings, your response is probably more appreciative and enthusiastic than it was before. I respond with words that reflect my joy for living and my appreciation for what I have and where I am going. Consider the difference this will make to your attitude, and the attitude of others toward you.

Be thankful for everything you listed, every day. Live every day with an attitude of gratitude. You have so much to be thankful for. And if you want more, you will have to give more. Get in the habit of giving more than you take. For example, if you want more compliments, you're going to have to give more first. So start thinking of ways of giving. Get actively involved in your community or in non-profit organizations and associations related to your type of work.

List some things that you could do to give of yourself.

_____

_____

_____

_____

_____

_____

You are worth a lot—more than you think. Take care of yourself, your health, your family and your friends. Remember, you are alive and you are important. Be thankful for that. Whatever you decide to do, do your best at it and continually hold, in your mind's eye, a picture of yourself successfully achieving your goals.

Remember to expect miracles…

Summary

Discipline # 12: Be Thankful

Before you can have more out of life, take inventory of your blessings.
Practicing thankfulness is about not taking life for granted.

How are you?

If you want more, you will have to give more. Get in the habit of giving more than you take.

You are important.

Expect miracles…

Thought space

_____

_____

_____

_____

_____

_____

_____

_____

_____

_____

_____

_____

_____

_____

Conclusion

Your living is determined not so much by what life brings to you as by the attitude you bring to life; not so much by what happens to you as by the way your mind looks at what happens.

John Homer Miller

You have completed the book. I hope you enjoyed reading it and doing the exercises as much as I enjoyed writing it. This is my way of being thankful for what I have learned, and giving back—sharing my knowledge and experiences with you so that you too may achieve your dreams and live life to its fullest.

What you think you are is linked to what you do. How you feel about yourself controls what your attitude will be. Your self-image, your self-respect and the manner in which you portray yourself to the world are very much a part of you. You are marketing and selling a product, and that product is you. You are responsible and accountable.

Commit to taking hold of your mind. Don't let fear or indecision stand in your way. Take control of your habits and your life. Accept responsibility to grow and develop. Never acknowledge the possibility of defeat.

Live with an attitude of positive expectancy, knowing that whatever happens in your life benefits you in some way.

Everything you have read in this book and all the exercises you have completed boil down to one thing: *attitude*. Attitude is a mindset. It is your outlook on everything. Your attitude will make or break you. Attitude drives everything.

The longer I live, the more I realize the impact that my attitude has had in my life. Attitude is more important than what other people think, say or do. It is more important than education, circumstances, success or failure. It is more important than skills, appearances or giftedness. It will make or break a person, a friendship, a family, a home, a church or a company.

The remarkable thing about attitude is that it is under our complete control.

We have a choice, at all times, about the attitude we embrace. We cannot change our past. We cannot change the way other people act or the things they say. We cannot change the inevitable. The only thing that we do have complete control over and can change is our outlook—our attitude.

You are in charge of your attitude. Make the best of it, for you!

Online for Life

The 12 Disciplines for Living Your Dreams

1. **Know your rights** because you have the right to your dreams, desires and expectations—to have what you want, to like yourself as you are, to change, to fail, to be imperfect, to choose, to ask, to decide how you will use your time and energy, and you have a right to lunch (when you pay for it).

2. **Make a decision** to do something about your life and live the life of your dreams, or to accept life as it comes. The first step in self-motivation is to make the decisions. The decision maker, and not the choice, makes the decision work. Making a decision is almost always more important than the substance of the decision itself. Conversely, making no choice—indecision—invalidates all options because it paralyzes you. There are three types of people in this world: those who don't know or can't decide on what they want; those who wish and dream and do nothing about it; and those who know what they want, plan for it, and go out and get it. Which one are you?

3. **Take control of your life** by controlling your thoughts and states of mind. Your thoughts control your attitude and how you

react to situations. Your thoughts are you! If you fail to control your mind, how can you control anything else? To take control of our lives we must first identify the things we have no control over and the things that we have or can control.

Your first step is to decide to take control. Rid yourself of externally and internally accepted baggage. Your beliefs drive your attitude. Your attitude drives everything! Become aware of what you are saying and what you are thinking, as your thoughts of today are your realities of tomorrow. If it is not the way you want it to be, reject it. Put a big solid red X through it. Stop it! Replace it with the way you want it to be.

Discipline yourself—do what you have to do even when you don't want to do it, and then reward yourself. Identify the habits that are working for you (effective) and those that are working against you (ineffective). Habits are not easy to break, and it takes up to 30 days to master a new habit. So start now! You will need commitment, discipline and determination to change your habits, but the rewards are worth it. Write everything out. Create a journal to refer to. Decide what steps you will take to take control of your life. Make a time and frequency commitment (discipline) to completing all the exercises in this book.

4. **Know yourself** or your journey into the future will be uncertain. Defining your identity will keep you focused as you later set priorities, organize tasks, deal with emergencies and accomplish challenges in your personal and business lives. Look inside; what do you see? Your identity and how you feel about yourself is most important. Who am I, without roles? What are my values? How do I see and feel about myself? What are my strengths and weaknesses? What motivates me? What *de*motivates me? What are my fears and how will I overcome them? IF I had the

courage to see myself as I really am, I would find out what is wrong with the way I am approaching life, and correct it.

5. **Know what you want out of life** by listing all of your dreams, desires and expectations as if nothing were impossible. What great thing would you attempt if you knew that you couldn't fail? How much time do you have left to accomplish what you want out of life? What are your retirement expectations?

How much time do you have prior to retirement? If you were told you had six months to live, how would you live them? How would you want your family, friends, and work associates to remember you? What would you want them to say in your eulogy? What behavior changes do you need to make to become the person in that eulogy? If a statue was built in your honor, what accomplishments would you want to have listed on the plaque?

6. **Group, categorize and prioritize** your dreams into time periods. Compare your dreams with the exercises you completed in the first five disciplines. The picture of yourself that you developed should be consistent with your most important dreams. Define your purpose: what do you want to be, do and have?

7. **Identify what you are prepared to give in exchange** for your dreams and desires. Expect to make changes in your life: in the way you spend your time, effort and money, and in your relationships, habits, education and career. Are you prepared to pay the price?

8. **Create a goal logbook.** A goal is an end, a result, not just a task to be performed. It describes the condition we want to achieve. Goals are an extension of your values. Goals must be

S.M.A.R.T. Ask yourself: Is this goal really mine? Is it morally right and fair? Are my short-range goals consistent with my long-range goals? Can I commit myself to complete the project? Can I visualize myself reaching this goal?

Create a goal logbook and address each of the following areas:

- State the goal, date for completion and outcomes expressed in sensory-based terms: the sights, sounds and feelings you want to experience.
- Identify obstacles you might meet, develop the contingency plans to overcome those possible obstacles, identify the skills and behaviors you'll need, and the people, groups or resources you can call on for help.
- Develop a detailed step-by-step success-oriented action plan with start and finish dates, and with a method of monitoring and measuring your progress.
- Create a system to recognize and reward yourself for doing what you indicated you would do along the way.
- Finally, make a commitment to yourself to follow through and do what you have to do.

9. **Commit to your action plan**, taking on the complete responsibility to "make it happen." Of all commitments, the ones you make to yourself are the most important to respect. To commit to something is to take a risk.

You can succeed if your willingness to leap overpowers your concern about what could happen if you fail. Avoid the regret of looking back on a life of opportunities not taken. Discipline yourself and do whatever you have to do for at least the next 21 to 30 days, no matter what.

10. **Be action oriented** and "do it now!" Don't expect to *find* time
    to achieve your goals, *make* the time. Determine your most pro-
    ductive time of the day and dedicate it to the most important per-
    son in the world ("I" time).

    Deal with the unpleasant, large or hard tasks first. Create a
    prioritized to-do list daily, weekly and monthly. Accomplish
    some piece of a major objective daily. Remove time wasters.
    Take care of yourself with exercise, a healthy diet and a bal-
    anced life. Every day, visualize, in detail, the end result. Change
    your behavior and you can change your feelings and ultimately
    your thoughts. Control what you say to yourself and how you
    think. Success breeds success. Don't ever give up on taking
    action. Make your dreams happen!

11. **Monitor and measure your progress** to stay informed on how
    you're doing. It will motivate you to keep going and to make the
    necessary adjustments along the way. The Goal Chart summa-
    rizes all the expectations and dreams that you intend to turn into
    reality. The Monthly Monitor Chart provides you with a 31-day
    habit-forming process for monitoring and measuring your
    progress. The charts remind, discipline, guide, monitor and
    reward you. They make you aware of your behaviors, pointing
    out where and when you should make adjustments.

12. **Be thankful.** Before you can have more out of life, take inven-
    tory of your blessings. Practicing thankfulness is about not tak-
    ing life for granted. How are you? If you want more, you will
    have to give more. Get in the habit of giving more than you take.
    You are important. Expect miracles…

Online for Life

"It is not the critic who counts; not the man who points out how the strong man stumbles, or where the doer of deeds could have done them better. The credit belongs to the man who is actually in the arena, whose face is marred by dust and sweat and blood; who strives valiantly; who errs, and comes short again and again, because there is no effort without error and shortcoming; but who does actually strive to do the deeds; who knows the great enthusiasms, the great devotions; who spends himself in a worthy cause; who at the best knows in the end the triumph of high achievement, and who at the worst, if he fails, at least fails while daring greatly, so that his place shall never be with those cold and timid souls who know neither victory nor defeat."

Theodore Roosevelt

Take Action

When you decide to live your dreams, discipline yourself and be the best you can possibly be. Reward yourself for doing it. Don't ever quit. No matter what, don't fall down—fall back, look up, see your dream, feel it and hear it. Get up, get over it and get Online for Life! Your dream is waiting for you...what are you waiting for?

Bob Urichuck

Bibliography

The Holy Bible. New York: The World Publishing Company.

Covey, Stephen. *The Seven Habits of Highly Effective People*. New York: Simon and Schuster, 1989.

Gleeson, Kerry. *The Personal Efficiency Program*. New York: John Wiley & Sons, Inc., 1994.

Hill, Napoleon. *The Law of Success*. Chicago: Success Unlimited, Inc., 1979.

Hill, Napoleon. *The Think and Grow Rich Action Pack*. New York: Hawthorn Books Inc., 1972.

Jeffreys, Michael. *Success Secrets of the Motivational Superstars*. Rocklin, CA: Prima Publishing, 1996.

Lakin, Alan. *How to Get Control Of Your Time and Your Life*. New York: The New American Library, Inc., 1973.

Lorayne, Harry. *Secrets of Mind Power*. New York: The New American Library, Inc., 1975.

Mandino, Og. *The Greatest Salesman in the World*. New York: Bantam, 1983.

Mandino, Og. *The Greatest Miracle in the World*. New York: Bantam, 1988.

Robbins, Anthony. *Unlimited Power*. New York: Fawcett Columbine, 1986.

Sandler, David H. *You Can't Teach a Kid to Ride a Bike at a Seminar*. New York: Dutton, 1995.

Sinha, Shall, Ph.D. *Words of Wisdom, WOW*. Alberta: SKS Publishing, 1997.

About the Author

Bob Urichuck is a respected professional speaker, trainer and consultant, working with individuals and organizations across Canada, the U.S., Europe and Asia. He is an expert on motivation, leadership, sales, recognition and team skills, and is a cultivator of human potential in all areas of personal and business life. Bob is also internationally known for "Why Sales People Succeed" and his "ABC, 123 Sales Results System," a non-traditional sales process (Bob's book on that topic is scheduled for release in 2001).

Bob is a Certified Sales Professional (CSP) and has been certified as a Master Trainer by Zenger Miller and Xerox Team Skills. He is the founding president of the Canadian Association of Professional Speakers (CAPS) Ottawa. Bob lives in his dream home on the shores of the Gatineau River at Mont Cascades in Cantley, Quebec with his wife, Joan, and sons, Michael and David.

Contact information for speaking, training, consulting, workbooks, charts, audio and video tapes and other products:

Bob Urichuck Management
BobU.com

Tel: (819) 827-2296 • Toll-free: 1-877-658-8224
Fax: (819) 827-1658 • E-mail: bob@bobu.com

To the Meeting Planner:

Bob's RESULTS-oriented approach means that he takes the time to truly understand your needs and those of your audience. When you hire Bob, he delivers a custom-designed program, not a "canned" presentation. Using a myriad of proven, interactive techniques, Bob propels both the team and the individual to commit to actions that lead to measurable results. Combine this with Bob's partnership approach to continuous learning and reinforcement, and you are guaranteed lasting results.

Thank you for the enlightening and motivating presentation. You helped us focus on the little things that matter most. You got the most skeptical to become believers by day's end—a great achievement! We accomplished more in one day with you than we ever did in the past. A big contributing factor was your passion, your beliefs and your "do it now" attitude.
Bombardier Motor Corp. of America, Claude J. Joncas, Regional Sales Manager/Northeast U.S.

We had almost 500 employees register for the 250 seats available. The mean score from evaluations for content, instructor (organization, professionalism, knowledge and interaction) and program impact was more than 4 out of a possible 5.

Nortel Networks, Aralia Ottawa EHS Canada, Pamela Davis

I was most impressed with all of the positive evaluations. But mostly, with all of the time you spent prior to the event to identify the association's objectives, specific needs and desired outcomes. I appreciated your suggestions, the resource material you distributed, and the follow-up after the presentation. I can honestly say I've never worked with a speaker who cared so much about the success of our meeting.

Canadian Professional Sales Association,
Anne Babej, Director, Professional Development

Despite the challenge of having to speak to an audience coming from diverse cultures and businesses, your candour and knowledge of sales made rapport and learning easy. The post-conference evaluations were extremely positive with several singling you out for Kudos.

Reed Elsevier (S) Pte. Ltd, Singapore,
Michael Tan, Director, Business Planning

Congratulations on your high ratings. The evaluations on your sales courses ranked Course Content 4.75/5 and Instructor Effectiveness at 4.89/5.

Singapore Institute of Management,
Corinne Lam (Mrs), Department Head, HRD Programmes B3

You are so dynamic that I noticed you have no trouble holding people's attention. You are knowledgeable, organized, articulate, and pace yourself to the learning level of the class. You make your audience very comfortable and that promotes good discussion. Your energy and enthusiasm are contagious and I can't wait to get out and sell, sell, sell!

Canada Post Corporation, Janie Burstein, Director, Government Sales

Live the Life of Your Dreams
The Interactive Multimedia Course

Live the Life of Your Dreams is the interactive multimedia version of the book *Online for Life*. The course is filled with graphics, video, narration and exercises to present you each of the 12 Disciplines to success. It is as if Bob is right there beside you every step of the way to coach and encourage you. This self-contained course can be run on most PCs and requires only minimal computer skills.

Live the Life of Your Dreams consists of fifteen modules. First you create a profile of yourself. Then, section by section, you will be presented with each of the 12 Disciplines to living the life of your dreams. By employing sophisticated programming techniques, the course dynamically creates special exercises based on what has been learned previously about you. A personality test helps you gain a greater understanding of yourself. When you have completed each of the modules, you will have created a dream logbook and action plans, and will be ready to measure and monitor your progress.

Live the Life of Your Dreams makes a great gift for a family member, friend or business colleague. Even after your first introduction to Bob's 12 Disciplines, you will continue to benefit. The CD-ROM provides a quick review when you need that extra bit of encouragement. It also provides an easy and efficient means to maintain and review your logbooks and monthly monitor charts. Through our Web site, the course is updated regularly with new features.

You can purchase your copy for $34.95* by phoning us or by visiting our Web site. Also inquire about the audio CD for just $9.95 when you purchase the course (regularly $15.95). To learn more about this product and view a demo, visit www.nairam.com/products/Dreams

Nairam Multimedia
P.O. Box 604, Station F, Toronto, Ontario M4Y 2L8 CANADA
Phone: (416) 204-9696 Toll-Free: 1 888 298-0776
Purchase on-line at www.nairam.com/shopping.

Please allow 4 to 6 weeks for delivery.
* A handling charge of $5.00 (per item) plus shipping charges
and applicable taxes will be included.
** Canadian residents add 7% GST; Ontario residents also add 8% PST

Minimum System Requirements

- Win 95, 98, NT, 2000
- 133 MHz PC
- CD-ROM drive
- Windows compatible sound card

- 800 x 600 resolution and 8-bit,
  256 colour monitor or higher
- 32 MB of available RAM
- 30 MB of available hard drive space

Books that inspire, help and heal

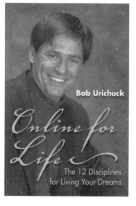

Bob Urichuck

We hope you have enjoyed
Online for Life:
the 12 Disciplines for Living Your Dreams

To order additional copies of *Online for Life*
by Bob Urichuck please contact Creative Bound Inc.
at 1-800-287-8610 (toll-free, North America) or
(613) 831-3641. Associations, institutions, businesses
and retailers—ask about our wholesale discounts for
bulk orders.

ISBN 0-921165-65-X $19.95 CAN
200 pages $15.95 US

Luke De Sadeleer

Vitamin C for Couples
7 "C"s for a Healthy Relationship

The Prescription:

- Caring   - Conflict
- Change   - Creativity
- Communication   - Commitment
- Connection

Practicing the 7 "C"s described in this book will help to
make a good relationship even better. Just as you take
Vitamin C to build up your immune system and keep your body healthy, a regular
dose of the 7 "C"s will bring you closer to your partner and keep your loving relationship strong.

Luke De Sadeleer, the Couples Coach™ is a professional speaker, author and facilita-
tor, encouraging people to take control of their lives and recover their passion.

ISBN 0-921165-68-4 $18.95 CAN
                       $14.95 US

Call to order: **1-800-287-8610** *(toll-free in North America)*
or write to: **Creative Bound Inc.**
Box 424, Carp, Ontario, Canada K0A 1L0

www.creativebound.com

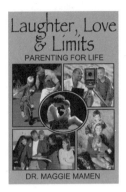